DEVELOPMENTS IN PRIMARY
MATHEMATICS TEACHING

Ann Elisabeth Sawyer

David Fulton Publishers

London

David Fulton Publishers Ltd
2 Barbon Close, London WC1N 3JX

First published in Great Britain by
David Fulton Publishers 1993

Note: The right of the author to be identified as the author of this work has been asserted by her in accordance with the Copyright, Designs and Patents Act 1988.

British Library Cataloguing in Publication Data

A catalogue record for this book is available fom the British Library

ISBN 1-85346-196-2

Typeset by Spectrum City, London
Printed in Great Britain by BPCC Journals Ltd., Exeter

DEVELOPMENTS IN PRIMARY
MATHEMATICS TEACHING

The Primary Curriculum Series

This innovative series promotes reflective teaching and active forms of pupil learning. The books explore the implications of these commitments for curriculum and curriculum-related issues.

The argument of each book flows in, around and among a variety of case studies of classroom practice, introducing them, probing, analysing, and teasing out their implications before moving on to the next stage of the argument. The case study material varies in source and form – children's work, teachers' work, diary entries, drawings, poetry, literature, interviews. The vitality and richness of primary school practice are conveyed, together with the teacher expertise on which these qualities are based.

Cover photograph: by kind permission of St George's C.E. First School, Kidderminster, taken by David J. Montague-Smith.

Contents

Introduction

The rapid introduction of the National Curriculum for Mathematics and its effect upon classroom practice is the main thrust of this book. My interest in these issues grew from my involvement as a member of the National Curriculum Working Party: Mathematics from 1987 to 1988. Prior to the introduction of the National Curriculum, there was no nationally agreed curriculum; no standardization across schools and LEAs; no agreement about what children needed to learn. Some schools used a commercially published scheme as the basis of the mathematics teaching, other schools devised their own curriculum, then used combinations of teacher-made and published materials. Some LEAs produced curriculum guidelines for mathematics, other LEAs believed that schools should devise their own. Some teachers formed curriculum development groups in order to support each other and to identify common ground for teaching and learning.

The introduction of the National Curriculum brought about changes. The statutory mathematics curriculum had to be implemented by primary schools. It contained topics, such as probability, which were largely unfamiliar. The inclusion of the use of calculators within the Orders for Mathematics meant that those schools which did not already use calculators would need to review their current teaching methods and consider how and when to introduce the use of calculators. The Logo examples in the Orders would highlight to many schools that since they did not use Logo, this was another area that needed to be considered. Attainment Target 1, Using and Applying Mathematics, implied a practical, investigative approach to mathematics which was new territory for many teachers, even though this approach had been advocated by advisory teachers since the publication of Cockcroft (1982). Many teachers were fearful of managing this curriculum, because of what was new or unfamiliar and because there was very little published support material available.

With the introduction of the National Curriculum schools reviewed their programmes for teaching mathematics. The case studies which teachers have kindly allowed me to use highlight the amount of work which has been undertaken in the past four years. In some schools there have been major revisions of the established curriculum, others needed to introduce a topic which was not taught previously. Some schools reviewed the suitability of the published scheme which they used, some purchased new ones. Some schools considered their resourcing policy, which led to the purchase of new materials and to considerations of suitable storage and access to materials. The publication of the Non-Statutory Guidances (NCC,1989; 1991) has also made an impact, as can be seen from some of the issues illustrated in this book – for example, children's attitudes towards their mathematics. Many of the teachers who contributed to this book were attending INSET courses for mathematics coordinators as their schools had highlighted the need for a member of staff to be trained as a coordinator. These courses raise the confidence of teachers and encourage classroom innovation.

There was the risk that teachers would see the National Curriculum for mathematics as the whole of the mathematics curriculum: what was required for children to learn would be all that was taught. Teachers were required to produce forward plans using the Programmes of Study, to log attainment targets, to record children's attainments. Children's own interests and enthusiasms, teachers' particular interests, could be lost because of the pressures to 'deliver' the National Curriculum.

It was exciting to find how much effect Attainment Target 1 has had upon teachers' intentions in their classrooms. Some of the teachers who have contributed concentrated upon the development of investigative approaches in their teaching. The children's reactions to this method of working have been recorded as have the changes in work habits, including improved confidence and motivation, cooperation and collaboration amongst some of the children. Others, it was noted, regarded cooperation as a form of cheating. This may reflect society's views of mathematics, which may in turn reflect past experiences of mathematics as a subject which was hard and which most people felt that they failed.

During the course of collecting material for this book, the

Alexander, Rose and Woodhead (1992) discussion paper, *Curriculum Organisation and Classroom Practice in Primary Schools*, was published. This raised the issue of topic work and single subject lessons as means of teaching. It has been possible to review different planning models which teachers have used in order to teach mathematics and to consider what the requirements are for effective teaching.

Assessment and record-keeping were raised by many teachers as major areas of concern. These are addressed in Chapter 7, with contributions from teachers across the primary age range. Concentration upon the assessment process by teachers has caused increased awareness of the importance of evaluating the effectiveness of planned activities in order to make decisions about the next stage of learning; assessment of children's attainment was not divorced from the planning and evaluation cycle.

It was encouraging to note the raised status of teachers of children in Key Stage 1. This can be deduced from the quality of the work which these teachers encouraged. They were the first to undertake the implementation of the National Curriculum and the first to be involved in formal assessment procedures, and gained much knowledge and skill which they used and continue to use to the advantage of their pupils and their colleagues.

There is still, in many schools, a shortage of computer hardware, and the use of the computer, often shared between classrooms, is still restricted. This may well explain why there was little evidence of data handling software in use by children. However, it was possible to find examples of the introduction of Logo, both through the use of programmable toys and of screen-based Logo. One teacher also introduced the use of concept keyboards in her teaching. She worked through a theme, but has clearly highlighted the mathematical possibilities in this mode of working.

The importance of involving parents in their children's mathematics was evident in some of the projects undertaken. One teacher developed home-school links through encouraging children to take investigations home for all the family to attempt. Some teachers involved parents through the development of maths trails, others used display in the school as a means of showing parents and others what had been achieved and the quality of the work which the children had undertaken.

The data collection for this book took place from 1990 to 1992. Some teachers wrote an account of an aspect of their classroom

4

work; some schools invited me to observe; some teachers agreed to be interviewed about their work. The schools chosen included small village, large urban and inner-city primary schools and first and middle schools, both rural and urban. These case studies cannot be regarded as representative of today's practice as so few schools have been included; they can serve, however, to highlight issues which are common to many schools.

There are so many pressures upon teachers and schools at the present time. The primary curriculum appears overloaded with so many subjects and so much content dictated through the Statutory Orders. It is with great pleasure that I include so many examples of good practice in mathematics teaching, much of which is regarded by the schools concerned as innovative and which will lead to further development within whole-school policies.

I am extremely grateful to all those teachers who welcomed me into their classrooms and to those who sent me their contributions. Some teachers are named at the introduction of their case studies, others have asked to remain anonymous and their wishes have been respected. My thanks to the children who have allowed me to include examples of their written work and to reproduce their discussions. Thanks also to the parents, governor and students who were interviewed. And, finally, thanks to my family and colleagues, for without their help and forbearance this would never have been written.

CHAPTER 1

National Curriculum Implications for Teaching and Learning Mathematics

In this chapter, the recent history of mathematics teaching and the research evidence are considered in the light of the changes which the National Curriculum has introduced. The introduction of the 1989 Statutory Orders, the subsequent decision to revise these in 1991, and the likely effects upon schools are discussed briefly as these issues are taken up in other chapters in more detail.

The story of the pressure for change in mathematics teaching goes back to the Great Debate, which began with James Callaghan's speech at Ruskin College in the autumn of 1976. Since then there has been wide public debate about what and how children should be taught, not just in mathematics, but across the whole curriculum. The public concern was about standards of performance in school work. The curriculum was said to pay too little attention to the basic skills of reading, writing and arithmetic and, in mathematics, was not preparing children for the world of work. It should be remembered that *Aims into Practice*, the Schools Council project (Ashton *et al.*, 1975), identified six areas of human development and saw the curriculum as developmental through these areas. However, Richards (1985) notes that from the mid-1970s greater emphasis was put upon the needs of society and how these could be met through the curriculum, rather than the needs of the individual; the beginning of this can be noted in *Primary Education in England* (DES, 1978), which was organized with a subject-based focus, and encourages a return to subject differentiation.

In 1978 the Cockcroft Committee was set up to report upon the teaching of mathematics in schools, with particular regard to the mathematics needed in post-16 education, employment and adult life. The report of the committee was published (Cockcroft, 1982) and made some specific recommendations, including the following:

- schools should encourage the involvement of parents in their children's mathematics particularly through explaining new processes
- children need to understand their mathematics rather than just learn by heart useful processes
- the range of styles of teaching which children should experience should be promoted to teachers
- teachers should encourage children to develop the processes necessary for mental calculations
- skills of estimation should be developed
- children should experience the practical work essential for the development of mathematical understanding
- the development of mathematical language skills is necessary as part of the learning process
- the use of the calculator as an aid to teaching and learning should be encouraged.

The report expressed concern that, in general, girls performed less well than boys in mathematics. Possible reasons for this were cited: teaching methods which favoured boys; boys were encouraged to be more independent than girls; textbook illustrations tended to favour boys; boys demand more attention from their teachers than girls. At conferences around the country, members of the Cockcroft Committee discussed the main issues in the report, raising awareness in the teaching profession. LEA advisory teacher teams were set up to encourage schools to take account of the Cockcroft Report's recommendations.

Primary Practice, a Schools Council working paper (1983) encouraged a subject-based approach to the management of the curriculum. This was followed with the Curriculum Matters series from HMI which considered the curriculum subject by subject; this had an impact upon teachers and how they viewed the curriculum. In *The Curriculum from 5-16* (DES, 1985a) HMI discussed the curriculum through the five issues of breadth, balance, relevance, differentiation and progression. These issues are now embedded in the National Curriculum.

The mathematics document (DES, 1985b) identifies five main

categories of objectives for successful mathematics teaching and learning. These are facts, skills, conceptual structures, general strategies and personal qualities. The sensible use of the calculator is mentioned, and it argues that teaching standard algorithms for long division is now redundant, as is the use of logarithms. The document also lists some objectives for children to have achieved at the ages of 11 and 16. This was an important step along the road to an agreed curriculum for mathematics.

The Schools Examination and Assessment Council (1990) published the results of a survey into children's performance in mathematics at age 11 and 15. Their conclusions, based on the evidence which was gathered by the Assessment of Performance Unit (APU) in 1987, are interesting. Areas discussed include the use of the calculator, mental skills, estimation and measurement, the use of Information Technology and problem-solving.

For calculator skills, APU found that over two-thirds of 11-year-olds claimed to use a calculator at school, and about half of them to have a calculator at home. Some evidence was found to suggest that the use of calculators at school may have caused an improvement in children's scores since the previous testing some five years earlier, in the APU's number concepts and skills tests. However, many 11-year-olds did not understand decimal displays on the calculator, and would revert to pencil and paper method if a decimal display occurred. The report makes the point that children need to be taught how to interpret the calculator display.

For mental skills, APU notes that the Cockcroft Report encouraged schools to reintroduce the development of mental skills. More 11-year-olds were using rounding up procedures to help them to calculate than had been the case in earlier testing. However, APU found that some children were attempting to use paper and pencil algorithms in their heads, which were inappropriate. The implication is that mental skills need to be taught through discussion between teacher and children, rather than through the traditional weekly mental arithmetic test.

In estimation, children performed poorly. There was a lack of appreciation of the size of standard units, and confusion between metric and imperial measures. Again, Cockcroft had recommended that schools should place greater emphasis upon estimation tasks; children need to acquire the skill of accuracy in estimation alongside those associated with accuracy in measurement. APU found that this was not happening.

It was noted that schools lacked sufficient hardware and suitable software for their pupils' needs for IT applications in mathematics. The evidence on group problem-solving showed that children liked this way of working and that one of its strengths was in the sharing of ideas. APU considered that group problem-solving experiences would lead to the development of children's reasoning and social skills.

The evidence from APU relates directly to the teaching and learning of the National Curriculum for Mathematics as it reports its evidence by Attainment Target title. The report finds an improvement in performance in shape and space and handling data from the 1982 data to 1987 data. There is a reported decline in number and algebra skills across the same time span, which must have implications for teaching contexts for National Curriculum topics. It is possible that the Cockcroft Report's messages about children's acquisition of number skills and the use of calculators had been misinterpreted, so that perhaps children had not been encouraged to develop a range of paper and pencil, calculator and mental methods of calculation.

Since 1987 teachers have been inundated with documents from DES, NCC, SEAC and now DfE. Many of these have been consultation documents which have invited responses within a very tight time scale. For the mathematics curriculum, the sequence of events from 1987 to 1990 was as follows:

1987

July	Consultation document for the National Curriculum
July	National Curriculum Working Group for Mathematics set up
December	Interim Report of the Working Group for Mathematics

1988

January	Task Group on Assessment and Testing report published
August	Final Report of the Working Group for Mathematics
October	Responses to the final report to be received by NCC
December	National Curriculum Mathematics consultation report

1989

March	Orders for the National Curriculum Mathematics laid before parliament
June	Non-Statutory Guidance for Mathematics issued
September	Year 1 children began National Curriculum Mathematics

1990

September	Year 3 children began National Curriculum Mathematics

This time-scale was very short. From July 1987, when the

consultation document for the National Curriculum appeared, until Autumn 1989, when Year 1 teachers began to use the National Curriculum Programmes of Study for Mathematics, were just two short, hectic years. There was some LEA training for teachers for the implementation of the National Curriculum, but this tended to be about National Curriculum terminology, not about interpretation of meanings within programmes of study or statements of attainment.

In 1989 the Department of Education and Science published *National Curriculum. From Policy to Practice* (DES, 1989b) which set out definitions of the new jargon vocabulary of the National Curriculum and described, briefly, what was required of teachers and when. In the same year, and before implementation of the National Curriculum in Year 1, HMI (1989) published a review of practice in mathematics. The review describes good practice in mathematics teaching and learning across the whole primary age range, and includes references to work on pattern and number, including mental calculations, the development of pencil and paper methods and the use of calculators. Reference is made to a shortage of hardware in schools so that, although scope for development of the use of the computer is identified as desirable, in practice it is not feasible without the resources being provided from outside the school's budget. Although the report is critical of about a quarter of the schools inspected, there is evidence of exciting, stimulating work from others. The production of the review using glossy, good quality paper, with a variety of photographic evidence of children at work, all in full colour, gave an added emphasis to the good quality of the work which the report praised.

The National Curriculum for Mathematics in primary schools was introduced in stages: Year 1 in 1989, Years 2 and 3 in 1990, Year 4 in 1991, Year 5 in 1992 and Year 6 in 1993. By September 1993 the whole primary phase will be taught within the framework of the programmes of study. In 1994 statutory assessment at the end of Key Stages 1 and 2, that is for years 2 and 6, will be in place. However, as the timetable for implementation of the National Curriculum took four years to complete, some schools decided to introduce the programmes of study earlier than required throughout the school, in order to help support the Key Stage 1 teachers and to aid familiarity with the process and content of the National Curriculum.

The National Curriculum was introduced in order to raise

standards. In the National Curriculum consultation document (1987b) it states, 'The Government wants attainment targets and the content of what is taught to reflect current best practice and achievement'. Within the programmes of study and statements of attainment for the 1989 National Curriculum there is reference to using calculators and computer databases. (The programmes of study within the Final Report of the Working Group contained further guidance, including the use of Logo, but this was 'lost' in translation into Statutory Orders.) The examples in the 1989 Statutory Orders suggest using Logo, calculators, mental calculations, simple Basic computer programs and databases. Although there is no legal requirement to use these examples as learning activities, they highlight to teachers the recommendations of the Cockcroft Report, and evidence of good practice from HMI and APU reports.

For primary schools the National Curriculum has brought about a widening of the traditional mathematics curriculum. Attainment Target 1, Using and Applying Mathematics, was devised to take a central role in the mathematics curriculum. The programmes of study offer opportunities for children to apply their knowledge, skills and understanding in problem-solving and enquiry situations, to communicate the results of that enquiry and to demonstrate their achievements with reasoning, logic and proof. These were not part of the traditional curriculum for many schools and have been aspects of mathematics teaching which needed to be included within a school's curriculum plan. For some teachers, this has meant a new approach to their teaching and the need to develop assessment strategies for using and applying mathematics.

There is an expectation that children will be encouraged to develop personal qualities that will stimulate positive attitudes towards mathematics. Within the Statutory Orders no mention is made of equal opportunities, of girls' traditionally poor image of themselves as mathematicians, nor of the needs of children from different ethnic groups and cultures, such as support for bilingual learners. No mention is made of the advisability of encouraging parents to be involved in their children's mathematics. All children in state schools have an entitlement to mathematics teaching which reflects the programmes of study.

The structure of the number system, place value, developing mental and paper and pencil methods of calculation, are included in the programmes of study. As has already been mentioned, the use of calculators is implied within the Orders. Nowhere within the Orders are algorithms for calculation prescribed and this empowers teachers to encourage children to develop their own methods of calculation, based upon mental, paper and pencil, calculator and a mixture of these methods and then to develop methods which do not require the aid of a calculator.

The introduction of algebra at Key Stage 1 has raised the status of pattern work. Traditional activities which involve copying, repeating, extending patterns using beads, coloured rods and interlocking cubes, are an essential part of the algebra curriculum at Key Stage 1. This work is extended within Key Stage 1 and beyond, to develop an appreciation of the importance of pattern in number relationships, and to the use of symbolic and graphical representations to express those relationships. However, teachers' and student teachers' own experiences of algebra at school were not always positive; as one returner to teaching put it, algebra 'was about x and y and I never understood it'. The detail of algebra in Attainment Target 3 has not been part of all primary mathematics curricula. The emphasis upon algebra in AT3 implies the need for teachers to receive support and INSET training in order to help them to develop their 'comfort zone' for algebra. As will be seen in Chapter 5, some teachers have used this opportunity to encourage children to explore pattern in a wider field of study, incorporating music, science and art and thus to encourage children to explore mathematical concepts and to develop their mathematical thinking through other curriculum areas. In the world outside school, mathematics is needed as a means of communication within everyday living: it is not compartmentalized, as it so often is at school and as the National Curriculum's structure may have implied, into one particular facet of living.

The use of Logo is described in the examples given in the Orders. Again, for many primary schools this is a new venture and one where teachers need support. As APU found, schools have a shortage of hardware: not all classes have their own computer and most primary schools do not have a floor-based turtle, which can be used for early Logo work. Children are expected to understand movement and to identify location through distance and angle. Transformation geometry is included, which is the study of translation, rotation and reflection in movement. Other aspects of the programme of study for shape and space require children to recognize the properties of two and three dimensional shapes, to be able to use these to construct those shapes, and to use knowledge of angle and symmetry properties in polygons.

In the programme of study for Handling Data, children are required to collect, record, process, represent and interpret data. This requirement has extended the use of data-handling methods, from the usual bar and pie charts, to the use of much more sophisticated methods, including Venn, Carroll and Tree diagrams and bar line graphs for discrete variables, frequency diagrams and scatter graphs. Software packages have been developed which help children to produce such graphs and which will also allow them to represent data in various formats, so that they can make decisions about the most appropriate for the task. Again, the shortage of computers in schools means that many children do not have access to such packages.

The study of probability has been included within AT5 for handling data. At Key Stage 1, this encourages links across the curriculum, as stories can be used to develop an understanding of possible outcomes of events through prediction. This is another topic that was not included within the traditional mathematics curriculum and one for which support is needed, not least in terms of suitable classroom materials for teachers and children.

The story of the development and implementation of the National Curriculum for Mathematics does not end here. By order of the Secretary of State for Education, the National Curriculum Council set up a working group to consider the suitability of the 1989 orders for schools. Below is the timetable for further change:

1991

May   Consultative document for revisions to the Mathematics curriculum published

December   Orders for the revised National Curriculum Mathematics laid before parliament
Revised Non-Statutory Guidance issued

1992

August   Revised orders come into force for Years 1,2,3,4,5,7,8,9 and 10

1993

August   Revised orders will come into force for Years 6 and 11

At the time of writing, the revised orders have been in force for half a term. However, many of the teachers who contributed to this book were already using the new orders so as to become familiar with the new format of the programmes of study and to assess their children's attainment. The new orders reduce the Attainment

Targets to five from fourteen: using and applying mathematics; number; algebra; shape and space; handling data. (Measures has been subsumed under number and shape and space.) The programmes of study are, in general, the old orders' statements of attainment. The purpose of the revision was to reduce the number of statements of attainment to be assessed; this has been achieved, but each statement now contains a wide range of experiences from the programmes of study. How effective this will be, in practice, remains to be seen, as teachers will need to collect a range of data about their children's performance, based upon their planning from the elements of the programmes of study. For example, AT Ma2/1a states: 'Uses number in the context of the classroom and school.'

> The programme of study includes
> Counting, reading, writing numbers to at least ten.
> Knowing that the size of a set is given by the last number in each count.
> Understanding the language associated with number.
> Understanding conservation of number.
> Making a sensible estimate of a number of objects up to ten.

Each of the elements in the programme of study for level 1 in the above example suggests a range of experiences from which evidence of achievement can be gathered. Without this range of evidence teachers will not be able to assess each child's performance for 'Uses number in the context of the classroom and school'. The implication is that the range of assessments that teachers will need to make has not been reduced by the new orders.

The implementation of the National Curriculum for Mathematics and the subsequent revision of Orders in 1991 have involved schools in much discussion, planning and monitoring. For many schools the process began before the National Curriculum came into effect, as teachers reviewed their mathematics curriculum and compared it with the Orders. As stated above, mathematics topics were identified that were not covered in sufficient detail or were new (examples of how schools dealt with this can be found in Chapter 6). Schools that used a published scheme as the basis for their mathematics teaching found that publishers produced supplementary materials for them to use; other publishers have since produced support materials, particularly for the new topics.

The review of the mathematics curriculum did not just include content; teachers considered teaching styles, grouping of children, and the items listed in the Non-Statutory Guidance (NCC, 1989) as:

the nature of mathematics
school policy and the National Curriculum
pupils' mathematical experiences
pupils' mathematical activities
pupils' records of their work
cross-curricular issues
assessment
recording pupils' progress
evaluation
staffing and resources
classroom management
(paragraph. 4.1)

Teachers re-wrote their policy statements to conform to these guidelines. However, policy statements are statements of intent which need to be enacted in practice within the classroom and for there to be successful implementation of policy statements there is a need for staff development. Coordinators for mathematics in primary schools have responsibility for identifying staff needs and formulating policies for staff development. Throughout this book there are examples from teachers who have attended INSET courses for mathematics, and who have then become involved in innovative practice within their schools, encouraging other teachers to identify the benefits of what has been trialled and then introducing such change into their classrooms. The discussion in staff meetings of benefits and pitfalls from the trialling of new curriculum material contributes towards the formulation of new policy statements for whole school development of, for example, the use of calculators, or IT within mathematics teaching.

The new requirements for the assessment of children's achievements have led to the development of policies for assessing mathematics. The range of evidence to be collected for each statement of attainment has already been discussed in this chapter. Further discussion, including examples of teachers' practice, will be found in Chapter 8.

However, the recent changes to the Orders have not changed the basic content of the National Curriculum for mathematics. Using calculators as an aid to solving number problems will be assessed at level 4, so that the APU finding that children could not interpret decimal displays has been taken into account in the new orders. The use of Logo is still described in examples linked to statements of attainment but has not been included within the programmes of study, which may well reflect the findings of APU and HMI that schools do not have sufficient computer hardware for all children to have ready access to computers. The interrogation of data within a computer database remains within the statements of attainment in AT Ma5 at levels 4 and 5, which supports the Technology programmes of study for IT.

Teachers have been profoundly affected by these changes. The amount of paperwork has increased considerably, with the need to record what is planned, what has been taught and to whom, to keep records of assessment attainments for each child. Informal discussions in staffrooms refer to high levels of stress amongst teachers and to how the job of teaching has changed, so that classroom teaching appears to be a minor part of the teacher's role. There is the risk that the National Curriculum will become a straitjacket with no room for any curriculum content which has not been included in the Statutory Orders nor for the children's and the teacher's particular interests.

In the early years following the introduction of the National Curriculum into schools, there has been continued pressure upon teachers in primary schools through a spirited political and educational debate on the place of subject work and topic approaches to curriculum planning and teaching. The publication of the Alexander et al. discussion paper (1992), which had been commissioned by the Secretary of State for Education, stimulated further debate. The discussion paper (paragraphs 62 to 72) calls for more subject teaching in both Key Stages 1 and 2 to ensure that each programme of study is covered effectively. It points to undemanding topic work, which has no clear aim, involves much superficial copying from books and offers little opportunity for progression. It refers particularly to the need for rigorous planning, which identifies the key teaching objectives. The discussion paper highlights evidence of good practice in the topic approach, where schools have adopted carefully structured topic frameworks for Years 1 to 6. It refers to a move away from topics which allow children to follow their own interests from a common starting point and identifies as good practice those topic plans which identify the sequential development of knowledge, skills and understanding from several subject areas which can be taught through the chosen topic. Alexander et al. regard this as a more effective model for curriculum planning than the open-ended topic approach, and report that virtually no primary school works solely through topics, with approximately 30 per cent of primary school work taught as single subjects.

However, many teachers of young children believe that children learn best without subject boundaries, so that there is true interdisciplinary enquiry. Bruce (1987) describes the early childhood curriculum as follows:

> The early childhood curriculum is constructed from three different elements. First, it concerns the child and processes and structures within the child. Secondly, it deals with knowledge: knowledge the child already has; and knowledge the child will acquire competently but with imagination. Thirdly, it brings the child and knowledge together, appropriately and relevantly, using the environment of people, objects or material provision, places and events. The key to the early childhood curriculum is to observe, support and extend. (p.65)

Bruce sees the child as of central importance, with the child's interests to be fostered through the child constructing his or her own meanings. This is a very different view of the curriculum from that suggested in the Discussion Paper. The National Curriculum, on the other hand, specifies what children must know, do and understand within the separate subjects and from level to level, thereby identifying the 'subjectness' of each subject area through key concepts.

Without attention being paid to children's interests, it is difficult to see how children's positive attitudes towards mathematics will be developed. The child who brings a treasured object to school to share with her teacher and the other children should feel that there was genuine interest and that her contribution to classroom life was valued. The following case study, from a teacher of Year 3 children, illustrates this point.

CASE STUDY

1. Valuing a child's interest

During a classroom discussion about styles of clock faces, Joseph commented that his mother had a very old grandfather clock at home. The clock's face had roman numerals, but instead of the traditional IIII for four, it had IV. Joseph was told by me that instead of using IV, jewellers used the four IIII in order to give balance to the appearance of the clock face. The next day Joseph brought a silver teapot into school, because the hall mark included roman numerals. All the children examined it carefully, using a magnifying glass. This was the beginning of a classroom display of items which contained roman numerals.

The whole class was fascinated by roman numerals. How had the Romans used them? Attempts to calculate using roman numerals soon showed how difficult it was and lead to discussions about place value in our number system. The children asked me if some time could be found to study roman numerals further. They wanted to find out what types of clocks and watches were in their homes, if these were analogue, whether these had roman numerals or traditional figures. I suggested that the children design some data collection sheets and that the information should be entered into a simple computer database. This was done and to everyone's surprise it was found that in each household there were examples of both analogue and digital watches and a clock or watch with roman numerals.

Some of the children came from families which had lived in the village for over a hundred years. Marie suggested that it would be worthwhile to visit the church graveyard and to collect data from tombstones. Her family had lived in the village for about two hundred years so she was eager to find family graves. I asked the children what data they wished to collect and how they would record it. They decided that they wanted to search for roman numerals and to find out how old people had been when they died.

We did not spend a great deal of class time on this project. The children designed their data collection sheets at school then asked their families to help then to complete them. Children took it in turns to work in pairs to enter data into the computer database. I wanted to be sure that everybody had the opportunity to use this facility. I was pleasantly surprised to find at the completion of this project that those children who had less developed number ability had improved understanding of place value.

Joseph's initial comment about his mother's clock was made to a teacher who felt confident enough in her ability to identify mathematical opportunities to allow this interest to be followed for a short period of time. All the children in the class were interested in roman numerals and had joined in the data collection with enthusiasm. National Curriculum programmes of study for parts of AT2, number, and AT5, handling data, had been included.

Sometimes it can be the teacher's particular interest that will spark off some unplanned work. The following is a report from a teacher of a class of 6–9-year-olds.

CASE STUDY

2. Tessellation and symmetry
I had been loaned a book which showed some examples of the work of Escher. I was fascinated by the pictures and took the book into school to show

the children in my class. I intended to use the pictures to stimulate discussion for about 15 minutes. Simon and his brother Matthew were eager to tell me that their father had a print of one of the pictures on his study wall. Cathy wanted to know how to draw such strange pictures. Hannah was fascinated by the tessellations. We talked for an hour. The children pleaded with me to be given some time to try drawing their own pictures after lunch. During lunch I thought about the extent of the children's interest and realized that I needed to harness it. At home time I suggested to the children that we planned some work on tessellation and symmetry.

The following day Simon and Matthew brought their father's picture into school; it had pride of place upon the wall in the classroom. I talked to the children about tessellation and we spent some time walking round the school, looking at brick patterns, floor tile patterns, and describing them. The next morning Cathy arrived with large sheets of paper on which she had taken rubbings of the family's new kitchen floor and wall tiles. A week later Hannah's father came to ask for a short lesson on tessellations as he could not believe that his young daughter was so knowledgeable.

The project continued, with the children finding how to make tessellating shapes starting from a plane shape which would tessellate. Soon, every available display space in the corridors was covered with rubbings of brick and tile patterns and of the children's own tessellations.

We studied symmetry and transformations. By the end of the half term all the children in the class had a clear understanding of rotational and reflective symmetry and could identify which plane shapes would tessellate and how to produce tiling patterns with those that did not, using combinations of shapes (AT4). Children had planned their own work, made decisions about the materials they felt appropriate to use and had communicated their results to each other (AT1).

Confidence to move away from what has been planned and the ability to identify the possible learning outcomes from a new topic were this teacher's strengths. The children were confident mathematicians, able to tackle something new which they perceived as exciting and worthwhile. Here the National Curriculum was not a straitjacket, but a framework within which the teacher was able to check back at the conclusion of the project, to show what the children had learned.

The National Curriculum sets a framework within which teachers are required to work; it does not, however, dictate teaching styles, classroom organization and management, topics or themes which teachers may want to use. This is important as it allows teachers and children the freedom to plan a map of the curriculum which takes account of individual children's needs and interests. How teachers have used this freedom will be considered in Chapters 2 to 5.

Conclusion

This chapter has considered the rate of implementation of the National Curriculum, the implications for schools in planning and developing policies and the effect that the National Curriculum has had in widening the traditional primary mathematics curriculum. A brief survey of some of the official reports has been included, which points particularly to findings from APU and HMI which support the inclusion in the National Curriculum of using calculators and the development of mental methods of calculation.

CHAPTER 2

Starting Points for Using and Applying Mathematics: Maths Trails

The suggestion from the National Curriculum Council that maths trails 'offer a way of beginning a structured enquiry into aspects of the local environment' (NCC, 1989) has stimulated interest in using such trails. Maths trails offer children opportunities to use their mathematics. In most maths trails some of the tasks will be closed ones, such as counting objects or naming shapes, others will be more open, where children may collect information during the trail which they use in extended tasks in school.

This chapter describes three approaches to trails in primary schools and the issues which arose. The three primary teachers, whose reports form part of this chapter, were members of the same INSET course for primary mathematics. During the course they agreed to visit their local cathedral in order to produce a maths trail which they could use with their classes and which would also be a useful resource for other teachers in their school. The teaching objectives were to:

- Help children to appreciate an important and beautiful part of their heritage.
- Enable the children to see the cathedral from a different viewpoint. Many of them had attended craft workshops there.
- Develop their knowledge and skills in the fields of shape, number and symmetry.

This chapter describes the work which followed with their classes. The case studies describe the planning, implementation and extension activities which followed the teachers' initial visits to the cathedral. The studies are:

1. Cathedral trail work from Years 2 and 3.
2. A trail for the Garden Festival of Wales with Year 6.

3. A school environment trail devised by a group of Year 4 and 5 slow learners.

CASE STUDY

1. Cathedral trail work from Years 2 and 3, by Sue Plant

The visit to the cathedral to compile the trail inspired us enormously. We worked together, pooling ideas and then trying to make them valid for each of three age groups: Years 1 and 2, 3 and 4, 5 and 6. On reflection, I believe that we expected too much from the children as the booklet we had produced had to be pruned during the day of the children's visit to the cathedral.

I teach in a primary school which has modern buildings, has 140 children and is in a rural setting. My class consisted of 31 Year 3 children and I had persuaded the Year 2 teacher that a maths trail around the cathedral would make a worthwhile visit for our two classes. She was amenable to this so 60 children and 10 adults were involved in the trail.

Planning

In the days before the visit, I had spent time with groups of children, going through the booklet we had produced and marking the questions which I felt would be best left until our return to school. On the day before the visit each child received a map of our area and was asked to find our village, the city, and to colour in what they thought would be the most straightforward route. We checked the distance (19 miles) and the direction (due south). I asked them to estimate the length of time that they thought the journey would take. These ranged from 30 minutes to two hours. We also reviewed some work done in the previous term on lines of symmetry and plane shapes. In the weeks before the visit we had spent some time with 2, 3 and 5 times tables (AT2) and on compass bearings.

The maths trail

The first page consisted of a simple map of the cathedral produced by the Hereford Diocesan Council for Education. The following represents a selection of questions from two sections. The other sections were about the South Transept and South East Transept, The Lady Chapel and North Transept.

Outside
Draw the eight points of the compass on the plan of the cathedral.
Which direction does the main door face?

Face the North Porch.
How many sides has each of the turrets on either side of the porch?
What do we call a shape with this many sides?
To the left of the porch on the North Transept is a round window.
Draw the window and put in two lines of symmetry.
Face the North Porch.
Go to the remains of the Chapter House.
Count how many strides it takes you.
Which directions did you travel in?
How many sides of the ruin can you see?
Estimate how many sides the Chapter House had.
Can you draw a plan of the original Chapter House?

The Nave
Stand in front of the altar facing West.
Estimate and measure the length of the Nave in two different ways.

Method   Estimation   Actual Measure

How many large pillars?
Estimate and measure the circumference of a large pillar in two different ways.
How many children can you comfortably fit in a pew?
Count all the pews. How many?
How many pupils would all the pews seat?
Find a kneeler with a pattern that has a line of symmetry. Draw the pattern.

The trail

For the day of the visit the two classes were divided into small groups to be supervised by ancillary helpers or parents; maximum group size was seven children. The adults had been given time to look through the booklet in order to be ready to give assistance to the children in their group.

On the day of the visit the children were given their booklet, the bus arrived at 9.15 am and the trail was underway. On the bus the children checked their estimates of the time taken to arrive at the cathedral. The child who had estimated two hours as the journey time realized after half an hour of travelling that we were nearly there and hoped that the bus driver would go really slowly to make his estimate closer!

Each group was given a starting point at a different part of the trail, to avoid jams. This worked well; we hardly overlapped at all. My group consisted of some above average ability children and three who often misbehaved. This was my challenge! We started at the North Porch where the work went according to plan. Children in other groups did not record that the window was symmetrical but recorded instead that the window was leaded.

It seems likely that the children in other groups and their adult leaders did not understand the mathematical language. They were asked to find two lines of symmetry. Perhaps the visual impact of the leading in the window was stronger than considering the meaning of symmetry.

The Chapter House proved more difficult. For example, we had asked the children to count the number of paces from the North Porch. Some of them lost count as it was over 200 and the 10-sided shape of the original building (now ruined) was difficult to see and to draw.

Measuring the nave was found to be an exciting part of the work as the groups had to find two ways of doing this. Their choices included strides, arm lengths, counting tiles, measuring pews and multiplying. Similarly, finding the circumference of the pillars encouraged the children to be inventive in their methods. Visitors to the cathedral were amused to see groups of children hugging pillars and then sitting in pews to be counted and multiplied.

One of the most rewarding parts of the day was the reaction of the parents involved, who had no idea that mathematics could be part of the life of the cathedral. One mother asked for advice from me before answering a child's query and commented that before that moment she had no idea what a line of symmetry was. The involvement of parents in this enterprise helped to foster the parent-teacher partnership.

Follow-up work

During the next day we held a 'post-mortem'. It was agreed that the group size needed to be smaller for the younger children. Groups of four would have taken account of their reading ability. The children had thoroughly enjoyed the visit and it had enabled me to observe children using their mathematical knowledge in problem-solving situations.

The tasks which were set were not problems in the sense of open investigations. Sue refers to problem-solving as children deciding upon the appropriate mathematics to be used in order to complete the task.

An extract from a report written by one of the children is shown in Figure 2.1.

This child understood the purpose of the visit. Note his use of mathematical language in the description. He refers to position (South East), to size (big windows, 11 strides around the font) to how many (12 figures) and to age (Henry Bather was 73.) He identifies pattern in the carpet. He was able to use his mathematical knowledge and understanding across the mathematics

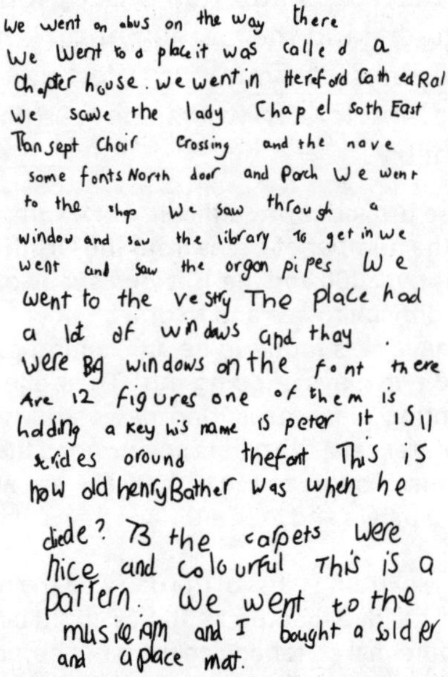

We went on abus on the way there
We Went to a place it was called a
Chapter house. we went in Hereford Cathedral
We sawe the lady Chapel soth East
Transept Choir Crossing and the nave
some fonts North door and Porch We went
to the shop We saw through a
window and saw the library to get in we
went and saw the orgon pipes We
went to the vestry The place had
a lot of windows and thay .
were big windows on the font there
Are 12 figures one of them is
holding a key his name is peter It 1511
stides around thefont This is
how old henryBather Was when he

died? 73 the carpets were
nice and colourful This is a
pattern. We went to the
musieqm and I bought a slider
and a place mat.

Fig 2.1 Child's written record of his visit to the cathedral

curriculum. This is the excitement of using maths trails: they
provide an integrated mathematics approach to teaching and
learning.

The cathedral trail was followed-up by a group of children being taken to the
local church. They were given the task of compiling their own maths trail,
using ideas from the previous one if they wished. They set off full of enthusiasm, carrying clipboards, measuring equipment and plenty of ideas.
The trail they produced was heavily weighted towards number but nonethe-
less reflects the amount of work that was put into the task. This is what was
produced.

A maths trail around St George's Church, Orleton
1. Look at the notice board outside. How many letters are there?
2. Find the grave of John Price. In which year did he die?
3. What shape are the panes of glass in the inner door?
4. How many figures are round the font?
5. How many pews are there?
6. How many children could sit in a pew?
7. How many children could sit in all the pews?
8. Count the heads on the wall. Divide this number by 3
9. Count the large beams in the nave. Multiply the number by 2.

10. How many organ pipes are there?
11. How many spans high is a pew?
12. Which different shapes can you find on the pulpit?
13. How many children could sit in the choir stalls?
    Multiply the number by 3.
14. Find the Remembrance Plaque. How long did the war last?
15. Draw one stained glass window. Draw in one line of symmetry.

Upon their return to school, the group was enthusiastic about the morning's work and the responsibility that they had been given. The next task was to produce the trail in leaflet form for other children to use. The group used the spirit duplicator to produce it and were delighted with the finished product.

The next group used this new trail. The delight for me was that whereas in the cathedral they had come to ask for reassurance, for instance:

Is there a line of symmetry?
Has a hexagon got five or six sides?

now the children seemed more self-confident, knew the names of the parts of the church without being reminded, and were happy to visit parts of the church to count or draw without the constant presence of the group leader. There was an improved degree of accuracy in counting paces, steps or spans.

I believe that maths trails such as these justify the amount of work involved because they demonstrate that mathematics is part of everyday life, not just something to be found in school. The work involved a range of mathematics programmes of study for Levels 1, 2 and 3, from AT 1, 2 and 4. The Cathedral trail opened the eyes of the children (and to an amazing degree, the parents) to the amount of mathematics that can be used in a place not normally associated with mathematics. From the experiences that the children in both classes had, I believe that these children could now set for themselves a maths trail in the classroom, the school environment, or in a town, and that the trail would be inventive and interesting as well as educational.

Some of the tasks set proved difficult for some of the children, for example, using larger numbers in counting. The achievement range across a year group is likely to be wide and it would be difficult to identify a selection of closed tasks suitable for this range. However, the inclusion of more open-ended tasks, such as finding how many children will fit into a pew, enables children to discuss the problem using mathematical language and consider how they will find a suitable solution. Adult help can be crucial in such a situation, to help the children to read the task and to encourage mathematical discussion.

The children who compiled their own trail used the experience of the cathedral trail. The tasks which they set were mainly of the closed variety and their recent work on times tables was reflected in the multiplication and division by 2 and 3. The responsibility of identifying questions for a trail, then producing the finished leaflets, which were used successfully by another group of children, must have improved the self-esteem of the trail compilers.

CASE STUDY

2. A trail for the Garden Festival of Wales with Year 6, by Pat Lloyd

Pat had been introduced to investigative mathematics processes during an INSET course in 1972. She had often felt like the lone wolf, the only member of staff to use these ideas in her teaching. In September 1991 she began another INSET mathematics course and found that it was 'a marvellous stimulating boost and very reassuring to know that the work I had been doing was on the right lines and not just something I had a bee in my bonnet about. It can be very difficult to stick to ideas and philosophies if you are always in the minority.' She reported as follows.

My concern, therefore, was not so much for my own classroom, but rather how to persuade other members of staff to at least try more investigative work, rather than just slavishly following the scheme maths and following-up TV programmes.

As a Year 6 class teacher it was more difficult to get in-depth investigative maths going if the children had little or no previous experience of the processes involved in such work. The school mathematics coordinator was eager that more of this type of work should be done. In previous years the head had asked that teachers should run 'project maths' mornings. The school had received a good input from the advisory maths team. However, the staff appeared to see the team's work more in terms of one-off activities rather than as an on-going process. Therefore, some other way of introducing this aspect of mathematical learning seemed appropriate.

The staff believed that practical and investigative mathematics took a long time to complete and that at the end of the task there was not always much to show in terms of recorded work on paper, in a maths exercise book or file; that is, no proof of achievement.

As part of my course, two course members and I made a maths trail around Hereford Cathedral. We tried to ensure that as many different aspects as possible of the maths curriculum were covered. At the same time much of the trail could only be done through investigation and much of that needed to be completed or followed-up afterwards, back at school. This made it part of on-going work, rather than just a one-off event. This seemed an ideal way for staff to begin to use investigations and not worry about covering their usual work, eg using non-standard measurements.

Unfortunately two members of staff had just taken their classes to the cathedral; they and other teachers had already made their plans for school visits during the summer term. I had to review my plans as full school curriculum and topic plans were already being made.

There had been great interest in the cathedral trail and many said that they would incorporate parts of it in future trips. Staff particularly liked the three levels of achievement within the trail. I worked on the principle that in a period of a constant battery of ideas on all aspects of an ever-widening curriculum, staff needed to know that something worked before they decide to launch into it. Rather than suggest that the cathedral trail was followed, I decided to incorporate a trail in my school visit to The Garden Festival of Wales. I would display the work gained from this at an open evening with the rest of the follow-up work, thus illustrating how well certain aspects of work can be covered in a practical day-to-day situation. I hoped to show the value of such work in the learning process.

A planning visit to the Garden Festival enabled me to identify ideas for the trail. I needed to bear in mind four main points:

1. The wide range of ability within the class (Year 6.) This was a factor which staff frequently raised. It needed to be carefully considered in all the practical work but more especially when working outside school if the tasks set were to be beneficial and enjoyable for everyone.
   The questions had to be stretching enough or have follow-up work back at school for the more able. There also had to be work which the less able could do, without it being obvious that this was just for them.

2. The number of children involved, in this case, was 31. The trail needed to take account of the fact that I would have two mother helpers with me. We needed to ensure that all the children knew what they had to do and were on task.
   With so many children to supervise the tasks had to be either simple enough to complete on the spot or simple enough in order to collect the information easily to do the work back at school. This would enable us to have enough time to make all scheduled observations.

3. On any educational visit, the children miss much of what was planned for them to observe. Conversely, they will observe and learn from unplanned observations.
   I planned to have several questions that could be worked on if the information required was not available on the day of the visit. Thus, children who had missed some of the questions would still be able to do much of the trail.

4. Careful planning for follow-up work in the classroom. Some tasks would need a different approach from that normally adopted, either because children had found it difficult or because there were new concepts, or for revisiting and consolidation.
   Not all the children would experience the same difficulties. Aspects such as average speed, area, volume and money needed work by many of the children. Most of the children in the class found it difficult (as I did) to estimate heights. By giving them experiences of standing

by a range of objects of different but known heights, such as the dismantling clock and man-made waterfall, I planned that the children would build up a store of comparisons in their minds.

This, then, was what was planned.

ITINERARY

GARDEN FESTIVAL WALES 1992

8.00	Depart School
10.00	Arrive Garden Festival Ebbw Vale
	Book in and walk to Funtastic Theatre
10.30 to 11.30	Funtastic Theatre 'Journeys'
11.30 to 12.00	Early lunch/snack
	Walk to BBC studio
12.00 to 1.00	BBC studio. Finish lunch in groups and visit Hoover Tent
1.00 to 1.30	Walk to Wetlands
1.30 to 2.30	Pond dipping
2.30 to 4.00	Wetlands to entrance via Hoover Tent (if not already visited)
	Down metal walk to Rainbow Theatre
	Electricity Maze

MATHS TRAIL

GARDEN FESTIVAL WALES

1. How many miles is it from school to the festival?
   What is that distance in kilometres?
   How long did the journey take?
   What is the average speed in mph?
   What is the average speed in kph?
2. Find out either by asking the hostess or by looking it up in the guide book back at school:
   a) the length and breadth of the festival
   b) the area the festival covers.
3. Find out the area of the festival that is covered by water.
   Work out back at school what percentage this is of the whole area.
4. If you have a watch, time how long it takes us to walk from the entrance to the Funtastic Theatre.
5. How many people do you estimate the Funtastic Theatre can hold?
   On what do you base your estimate?
6. How long, wide and high do you estimate the Funtastic Theatre is?
   If you have a chance, pace it out or ask one of the theatre group if they know.
7. What is the basic shape that the Welsh Water Pavilion is based on?
   How many of these would you need to make a complete one?
   Make one back at school.
   What smaller shape can you see in the larger one?
8. How much would it cost for us all to have:
   a bacon sandwich and a doughnut and a coke?
   (Collect the prices and work it out at school.)

9. How many people could sit down in the refreshment area at one go? If the people from 2 tables move every 10 minutes and new people fill their places, and the area is open for 10 hours, how many people could sit there in that time?
10. How long does the BBC broadcast from their studio every day?
11. How many steps (stairs) from the BBC studio to the Wetlands? What shape is each step?
12. Look at the pond creature models. How much larger than real life do you think they are?
13. How small are we shrunk to, to go through the Hoover tube?
14. How high are the carpet tufts?
15. How would you describe the size of the model of the grain of pollen?
16. What shape is the Hoover Tent?
17. How many steps are there down the metal walkway? Find out what height the walk-way covers.
18. What shape do the supporting girders make?
19. Find out how many plants were needed to make the flower rainbow.
20. How high is the man-made waterfall?
21. What shape is the Rainbow Theatre?
22. Estimate the width. What do you call this?

Results of the maths trail

As predicted, the children missed quite a lot of the trail. Not all missed the same points so that other children helped those who had missed something to fill in those details. The follow-up work went extremely well. It was a delight to see how much easier the children found the workings of average speed when they could relate it to the coach journey. The idea of area took on a new dimension when the children could look over the Valley of Ebbw Vale and actually see the area that the festival covered. The same applied to the percentage question...and so on through all the questions in the maths trail.

Many mathematics textbooks contain work on aspects of measures which use large numbers, for example, questions about journeys and distance, or finding areas of large tracts of land. Concepts of area, or average speed, when taken out of context, have no meaning other than a number, unless there have been other experiences which have allowed the child to estimate, to check that with measurement and to internalize that information. To identify a measure in context, such as seeing the area covered by the garden festival, enables children to make comparisons with that experience when estimating the area of another piece of land. The 'intuitive assessment of quantity', the term used by Williams and Shuard (1987), forms an essential role in accuracy of estimation, which in turn, is a necessary life skill.

The Welsh Water Pavilion was based on pentagons that were in fact slightly convex. At school, a group of children made a very large dodecahedron and its baby brother. Some of them worked on to find a net and size of angles. I was thrilled with this as this group insisted that no help from me or books was required because of the work we had covered in science (spokes at different angles from the centre of a circle) and the work they had done on Logo. (Much sweat and tears from me over Logo, but it is obviously reaping rewards.) Other follow-up work included a cartoon-type frieze, showing a bus illustrating average speed. All the children wanted to set up beefburger stalls after their market research into how many people they estimated would sit in the refreshment area and how much they would spend on coke, sandwiches, etc.

New challenges can be developed from the classroom tasks. For example, the children could be challenged to produce some simple costings for buying the food needed for the refreshment area and to estimate how many beefburgers, cans of coke, etc, would be needed, how much these would cost, how much profit could be expected. Or the challenge could be a development from this, into considering costings for an education visit, or for a class picnic. These are challenges which have no 'right' answer; children can make decisions and evaluate the results of the decision-making on the proposed outcomes.

Whilst this work was going on in my classroom, another member of staff devised his own maths trail based on the local parish church. Another member of staff in the infant department was very excited to find a published maths trail and wants to try it with her children because it exists! This is an aspect that I had not previously considered. As well as my setting the example, staff probably prefer to try something initially that has been worked out for them as they lack confidence in their own ability to devise their own maths trails.

I have been fired with enthusiasm for this work and have no doubt that this will catch on in school next year. At staff planning meetings I shall mention how exciting it can be and shall definitely include a maths trail either in my maths work or in project work. I hope that staff will see more clearly that a maths trail is not just work done on paper. Perhaps starting points for others might be smaller, less ambitious trails.

To find other teachers taking an interest in an innovative project and then to witness them take on the ideas within their own classroom is rewarding in itself. The processes and skills in the Programmes of Study for AT1 are developmental. Both short investigatory activities and longer ones, to which children return over a period of time, are needed to help children to develop these skills and processes. Other teachers within the school observed that what was happening in this Year 6 classroom was worthwhile and was achievable by their classes.

CASE STUDY

3. A school environment trail devised by a group of Year 4 and 5 slow learners, by Alison Parker Morgan

I teach in a rural primary school, with 95 children and five members of staff. My class last year consisted of 17 Year 4 and 5 children. I knew that I would have a final-practice student teacher with me for the summer term. The student would teach the majority of the class which would offer me the opportunity to work with a group of Year 4 and 5 boys who experienced difficulties with number concepts.

If this was to be successful it would be important that the boys experienced work of a practical nature with a minimum of recording. I chose to develop a mathematics trail with them. I had already worked with other teachers to devise a trail around our cathedral. We had been surprised at the amount of mathematics that we were able to utilize for our trail and I wanted to try this again, this time with my class. This would be a new experience for the children. It would also be a new experience for the school as nobody had tried this before; I wanted other members of staff to either use the trail which we would devise or to feel motivated to make one with their classes.

My reasons for choosing to use a mathematics trail were:

1. To give a small group of boys who experienced difficulty with mathematics the opportunity to use their mathematical knowledge in a relevant way and for them to realize that mathematics is used in everyday situations.
2. To give the children the opportunity to use their initiative and to be in charge of the content of the trail.
3. To incorporate as many aspects of shape and space (the mathematics topic for the first half of the summer term) as possible.
4. To ensure that the resulting trail was either relevant to other teachers' situations or appeared relatively easy to have made in order to encourage others to try this way of working.

I chose the school environment for the trail. This had definite advantages: there were no transport costs involved; small groups would be able to follow the trail with minimum supervision; the children would be in sight of the classroom at all times; the children were used to working in small groups around the school so this would be a familiar way of working.

Planning was relatively easy. The equipment we used was metre sticks, trundle wheel, clipboards, paper, calculators, pencils and rulers. The children were to suggest ideas. I was just going to guide them.

Once I had explained what a maths trail was the boys were keen to start at once and they rushed round gathering the equipment. We started work at the main entrance to the school.

Teacher: Is there anything we can count here?
Child: Yes. The slabs
Teacher: How shall we count them?

They started by estimating. Their estimates ranged from 40 to 70.

The children's estimates lay between a quarter and a half of the actual number of slabs, which was very inaccurate. More experience of estimating and the comparison of the estimate with the measure or calculation would help these children to become more accurate in estimating quantities.

Paul thought they should count them. He counted one row and found that there were 19 slabs. David decided he needed a calculator.

Teacher: Why?
David: So that we could add 19 eight times.
Paul: That's 8 lots of 19. We could times them.

Paul understood that repeated addition could be replaced by using multiplication; he demonstrated his understanding. Did David understand Paul's suggestion?

The next suggestion was to look at the shape of the slabs. That was easy, they were all square, but Paul measured just to make certain.
The children responded positively to the practical nature of the task. They thought through the questions. In a class situation they tended to 'turn off' and leave the thinking to other members of the class.
At the netball court I asked if they knew what the perimeter was, and someone did! One child measured one side.

Paul: We don't need to measure the other side. It will be the same. Now we need to measure that [the narrow] side and double it.
             (It measured 20m by 12m)
David: That's 20 + 20 + 10 + 10 + 4. That's 64.

I was pleased. His computation was both logical and quick.

And David demonstrated that he was able to break down the task into manageable chunks. Note that 12 + 12 becomes 10 + 10 + 4. He has developed a mental strategy which allows him to transfer parts of quantities in order to make the task more manageable.

Having measured the perimeter we looked at area. We started off by marking square metres in chalk on the court. The boys were soon convinced that it was unnecessary to draw metre squares all over the court. Adam suggested that we could times 12 by 20 on the calculator, which he quickly did. We carried on around the trail with the same high level of enthusiasm.

Towards the end of this work we had arrived at a point facing the field. One of the boys suggested counting the daisies - he was joking! Then another suggested that we counted the daisies in a square metre. The previous day's marking-out of square metres had made an impression. The boys headed off for the far side of the field where the daisies were densest. They surrounded an area with metre sticks and started to count. They quickly became confused and decided that there were too many daisies. They found another patch with fewer daisies and all started counting at once. Again, this proved to be confusing. Their solution was to elect one child as daisy counter and that closed and open daisies were to be counted. This proved much more successful.

We finished off the trail by adding up the numbers on the number plates of staff cars. Neil was not sure which numbers we were looking at to begin with. We had a discussion about which car had the highest number and which the lowest. One child noticed that one car had the numerals 384 and another 394. This led to a discussion about the difference between them.

When the time came to finish for that day the children wanted to carry on. They demonstrated a great sense of achievement and I was delighted with the way that they had worked. They had covered much more maths than they would have done in an equivalent length of time in the classroom; they had also demonstrated their understanding of topics which we had covered in the classroom and other areas had been reinforced.

I was undecided about whether to let the children write up the trail themselves or whether to word-process it. They had all written down the questions as we went along, but their spelling was very poor and if asked to re-write to make a good copy they would still make many mistakes. It was important that this work was successful for the children concerned. I wanted the rest of the class to find it visually attractive, so it was word-processed.

The trail

SHAPE AND SPACE MATHS TRAIL

Stand at the main doors and face South.
Look at the slabs
1. Estimate how many slabs there are.
2. Now count the slabs. How did you get your answer?
3. What shape are the slabs?
   Now look at the flower bed.
4. What shape is the flower bed?
5. Find 4 different symmetrically shaped leaves.
6. Find one leaf that is not symmetrical.
   Look at the bin on the left of the flower bed.
7. How many sides has the top got?
8. What do we call this shape?
9. What is the shape of the bottom of the bin?
   Walk round to the netball court.

10. Measure the perimeter.
11. Find the area.
    Look at the shapes on the netball court.
12. What shapes can you see?
13. How many rectangles can you see?
14. On a separate piece of paper, draw the netball court to scale.
    Face North. Walk to the end of the tarmac.
15. Measure from the corner of the tarmac to Class 4's door.
    Look at the bricks on the wall.
    The bricks TESSELLATE.
16. Draw the brick pattern.
    Look around you.
17. Draw two more patterns that tessellate.
    Walk West through the gate. Face North and look at the shed.
18. Draw the shed window.
19. Draw a line of symmetry on your drawing of the window.
20. Can you draw another line of symmetry?
    Face West. Walk past Class 4 and look at the shed in front of you.
21. What shape is the back of the shed?
    Still facing West look at the hedge along the Western edge of the field.
22. How many trees are along that hedge?
23. What shapes are most of the trees?
24. Count how many daisies in a square metre.
    Turn left and face South. Walk towards the car park.
25. Stand in a safe place and add up the registration numbers on the rectangular number plates on the teachers' cars.
    Walk quietly back to your classroom.
    By Neil, David, Paul and Adam.

Using the trail

The other children in the class used the trail. Each group was eagerly led by one of the boys who had designed the trail. I was fortunate to have the help of the student teacher so that we were able to closely supervise the groups. The children really enjoyed the work. A week later the children from Years 3 and 4 used the trail with their teacher and a classroom assistant as helper. They took two sessions to complete the work. Their teacher reported how pleasing it was to see the amount of work covered in this way.

Evaluation

The group of boys who devised the trail had used their mathematical knowledge in everyday situations. The children were able to pose and solve problems in a familiar situation. I was satisfied that the boys' response to their work demonstrated that they had achieved Ma AT1/3a and b as they had posed and solved problems in a familiar situation and used and understood mathematical terms and language. They had also covered work at Level 3 in ATs 2 (number) and 4 (shape and space.)

The children had benefited from my undivided attention for the hour and a half that it took to devise the trail. The input from the children showed that their understanding of some aspects of the mathematics which we covered in making the trail was better than I had previously thought. The boys gained confidence from the experience; they enjoyed being in a position of leader and to be able to assist others.

Copies of the trail were passed on to other members of staff, two of whom showed a great deal of interest. The trail was developed for my children, so that it would need to be adapted to suit KS1 or Year 6. The teacher of Year 3 and 4, who used the trail with her class, found that it helped her to become confident to design trails specifically suited to her children's needs.

The initial planning of the trail was simple. I wanted the children to devise the questions for themselves. I guided them; I found that I needed to do this more than I had originally planned in order to ensure that the trail had plenty of variety.

Using the trail with the whole class identified area as a topic which needed reinforcement. Some children misunderstood perimeter to mean area. The more able children found the trail relatively easy and finished it quickly and accurately. Those who gained most from it were working at Levels 3 and 4. For example, one child wrote:

I estimated how many slabs there were 140 slabs there were actually 152 slabs. We counted the slabs down each side and we did 8 x 19 = 152.

This child produced an estimate which was very close to the actual number of slabs.

She also perceived that multiplication of the number of slabs along each side would give the total. This child understood the procedure and was able to use it correctly to solve a problem.

She also used, correctly, the standard algorithm for addition, to find the total of the car numbers (see Figure 2.2)

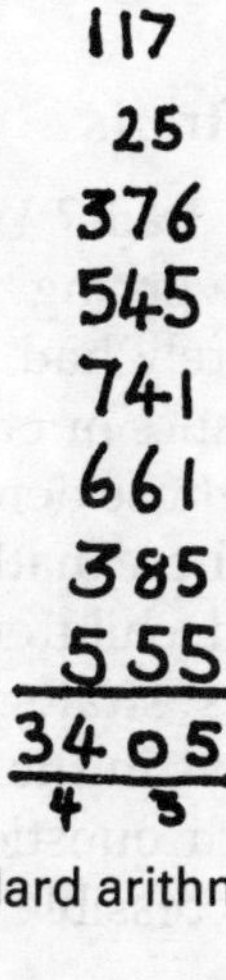

$$
\begin{array}{r}
117 \\
25 \\
376 \\
545 \\
741 \\
661 \\
385 \\
555 \\
\hline
3405 \\
\end{array}
$$

Figure 2.2 Use of the standard arithmetic algorithm for addition

Here the size of the total was much greater than in the slabs task. Were the numbers too large for her to attempt to make a rough estimate of the total? Did she have any strategies which would allow her to make a rough calculation in her head? For example, rounding to the nearest hundred would give $100 + 0 + 400 + 500 + 700 + 700 + 400 + 600 = 3400$. This would be a useful strategy to use either to give an estimate before calculating or to use as a check of the appropriateness of the size of the answer.

> I believe that this (successful outcome) was because it had been produced by children who were also working at these levels. Having the extra support of the student teacher ensured that we had effective supervision and support of the groups. I and the Year 3/4 teacher found that this work enabled us to observe the children's problem-solving capabilities closely.
>
> Follow-up work included other groups of children devising their own maths trails for others to try. The experience of having followed a maths trail had given the children examples of the types of questions which they might include. Copies of the resulting trails have been given to all members of staff as a resource.
>
> I shall be teaching a group of Year 1 and 2 children for the next school year. I intend to involve these children in a maths trail around school based on estimating and measuring. There will be a central display of their work for parents and staff to see the amount and variation of practical mathematics involved in following a trail.

Again, there were positive developments resulting from this project. Other teachers became interested in using a project approach which offered opportunities to assess the children's levels of knowledge and understanding, particularly within the problem-solving process (AT1).

The benefits of using maths trails

Why have schools used maths trails? What are the benefits and implications of this method of working? Desforges and Cockburn (1987) showed that children rarely had the opportunity to tackle real problems in their mathematics or choose strategies and skills for problem-solving other than those demanded by the worksheet. Whilst many of the tasks set in these maths trails were of the closed variety, some of them offered children opportunities to make decisions about the mathematics, strategies and skills to be used in order to find solutions. The boys in the third case study set their own tasks, they decided which questions to pose. As the case studies show, maths trails are accessible to all children at their level of operation and all the children involved, whatever their age or ability, found this a satisfying experience.

The opportunity to use mathematical knowledge and understanding in real-life situations helps children to see mathematics as a useful tool, as a means of communication and as an integral part of the real world. It also offers opportunities for the different mathematics topics of number, algebra, shape and space and handling data to be used in an integrated manner in order to solve a particular problem. Many children, mathematically educated on a diet of published scheme activities, will have experienced using aspects of mathematics in problem-solving situations, but not in an integrated manner.

Love and Tahta (1991) show that the term 'problem-solving' can mean solving a real mathematical problem or it can refer to a set of approaches to solving problems which teachers teach. From the above case studies it would appear that both approaches are appropriate in maths trails. Children can use their mathematical knowledge and understanding and the range of problem-solving strategies which they have acquired in order to solve real problems. Some of the tasks set will be of the closed variety, that is, there will be one solution. For example, from the first, cathedral, case study:

Draw the eight points of the compass on the plan of the cathedral.
Which direction does the main door face?

These are straightforward instructions, which the child either can or cannot carry out successfully, depending upon previous experience. It enables the teacher to assess a child's use of a skill (using a compass to identify direction) and to interpret that in a drawing. However, a task which needs children to use their mathematical knowledge, skill and understanding, if it catches the imagination, will produce more exciting work and can act as a starting point to further investigation. The following was a case in point:

What is the basic shape that the Welsh Water Pavilion is based on?
How many of these would you need to make a complete one?
Make one back at school.
What smaller shape can you see in the larger one?

The first question is closed; the second may need some investigation. The third, however, acted as the catalyst, sparking further interest: how to make a net, what size angles were needed for each component pentagon. This was a mathematical problem, which involved children in:

using their mathematical knowledge and understanding
communicating through talking, recording systematically, presenting their results to others in an understandable form
making and testing predictions, hypotheses, forming generalisations. (NCC, 1989).

Maths trails offer the teacher the opportunity to assess the children's achievements in AT1. The statements of attainment identify developmental strategies, and assessment of achievement in one activity can identify different children operating at different levels. Thus, open problem-solving activities in maths trails can be used for differentiation by outcome, whereas the closed variety can be used to assess what children can do. The trail needs to be carefully designed, either to contain a range of activities within which all the children involved can find success, or, if there are different strands of the trail, differentiated by task in order to take account of the range of ages and abilities within the group using it.

The third (school environment) trail offers a useful model for other teachers. Whilst it is recognized that it is not always possible for the class teacher to find the time to spend with a small group, the results of the experience for this small group were of great benefit to them. The boys had the opportunity to demonstrate their mathematical knowledge and understanding and their effective use of problem-solving skills and strategies. They were able to devise a trail for others to follow and to lead groups of other children around this trail, which in itself, helped to raise their self-esteem. Most important of all, their confidence in their abilities as mathematicians was raised.

Maths trails can encourage children to improve their personal qualities. These can be summarized as:

Motivation. The child wants to attempt a new task which may be unfamiliar.
Flexible and creative thinking. The child searches for ways forward, particularly when strategies already applied have not proved successful.
Perseverance. The child continues to work at an extended task, even though there may well have been set backs and new ways forward need to be found.

Accuracy. The child uses strategies to ensure, as far as possible, that the work produced is accurate.

Independence. The child shows independence of thought, perhaps trying different routes from others in the group.

Cooperation. The child works with others within a group.

Collaboration. The child takes an active part within the group, where the children may have decided to share out tasks or to work in pairs, each pair trying a different strategy, in order to find a successful route.

(NCC, 1989)

Children who have used a maths trail, have understood its purpose and can then move on to design their own trail for other children to try, will have demonstrated many of the qualities listed above. It is to be hoped that they also develop a positive attitude to mathematics. To achieve this success a number of factors need to be considered, and these are discussed below.

Planning

a. *The purpose of the trail.* Will it be mathematical or involve other elements of the curriculum? Is it to be used for teaching new concepts and skills? Will previous experiences be reinforced? (for example, the comparison of the children's heights with structures at the Garden Festival.) Which conceptual structures will be involved? Will there be opportunities for children to use their mathematical knowledge and understanding in order to solve problems? Which problem-solving strategies and skills will children need to be able to use in order to make effective use of the trail? Which personal qualities will the trail help to foster? Will children be encouraged to work cooperatively and collaboratively, to be independent, to show motivation and perseverance? Indeed the planning of a trail needs to take account of the classification of mathematical learning into the five areas laid out by Cockcroft (1982): facts, skills, conceptual structures, general strategies and personal qualities.

b. *Planning for assessment.* What can be assessed through the trail? Winteridge (1989) states that clearly identified expected outcomes are needed if children's learning is to be assessed. Where children are encouraged to use strategies and skills, there may be opportunities for assessing unexpected outcomes. The major feature of this way of working is the opportunity it gives for teachers to observe their children using problem-solving strategies and skills within their use of number, algebra, measures, shape and space and handling data. The assessed outcomes recorded within the case studies identified not only what children knew and could use, but also topics where further experience would be required.

c. Suitable content within the trail. Will there be one trail for all the children to use? If so, the range of abilities within the group will need to be taken into account so that a variety of tasks can be included which will ensure that there is work suitable for all the children. In the first case study some of the activities were too difficult for some children (for example, counting paces from the North Porch to the Chapter House, which involved numbers of more than 200). Decisions need to be made about how much of the work will be undertaken during the trail, how much will be information-gathering for further investigation back at school, and whether some children should concentrate upon particular aspects and share the information gained with others back in the classroom.

Trails consist of both closed questions, of the data-gathering variety (How many? Where? What size?) and of the open-ended, extended variety with further investigation back in school, such as the further investigation of pentagons, dodecahedra, nets and angles from the Welsh Water Pavilion. Planning should take account of resource needs for further investigatory and problem-solving work in the classroom. The availability of suitable computer hardware and software, such as a database and spreadsheet program, and of information and reference books, which will allow the children to follow-up observations in order to gain further information, can enhance the learning experience for the children.

In the first two trails documented in this chapter, the teachers planned for different starting points for the groups of children. If there are many groups of children this is a valuable strategy, avoiding the children competing for the same piece of information or wasting time waiting to begin.

Trail location

The trails recorded in this chapter were set in the school grounds, within the locality of the school (the church trail), and a coach journey away (both The Garden Festival of Wales and Hereford Cathedral). Schools which have successfully tried maths trails will sometimes incorporate them into educational visits. A description of such a visit, which incorporated a maths picnic, trail, treasure hunt and orienteering exercise can be found in Lloyd-Jones (1992).

a. *The school environment.* There are many advantages to this. It is a free resource (no coaches needed, for example); it is always available; it is well-known so that preparing the trail will be relatively straightforward; and it is a resource where it would be possible to devise a range of trails to take account of the changing seasons and to use different aspects of the environment. Children can frequently be supervised for working in this environment by parent or ancillary help. The inside of the school and, indeed the classroom, can be used as well as the outside.

b. *Educational visit, to a place of interest, or into the local town or village.* This will need careful planning, to ensure that the LEA guidelines for school visits have been adhered to. Children will need careful, constant supervision, which often enables parents to take part in a worthwhile school activity. Time for a visit to the chosen venue to prepare the trail will need to be found.

Preparation for the trail

It is essential that the adults who accompany the children are familiar with the concepts, skills and strategies which the children may wish to utilize. The teacher will find it advantageous to have a session with the other adults concerned, before the day of the trail. Suggestions of strategies which children might adopt, examples of questioning techniques which encourage children to search for possible solutions, rather than 'telling' the children the answer, can be introduced. This would be an excellent opportunity to encourage mathematical talk, to encourage the use of mathematical vocabulary. The Do Talk Record framework, from the Open University course (EM 235), offers opportunities for children to be involved in an 'effective mathematical situation' (Brissenden, 1988).

From the experience of the teachers using the cathedral trail, thought needs to be given to the size of each group of children. It would be helpful to consider the readability of the trail instructions and compare this with individual children's reading and comprehension ability. Adult helpers can act as interpreters of the questions for children who are not yet able to read and understand the questions for themselves. Another consideration will be the make-up of groups. Will children be placed in mixed ability or similar ability groups? If mixed ability grouping is used, then more able readers will be able to help others. No children should be in the position of being unable to take part in the work of a maths trail because they are unable to read the questions.

Staff development

Two of the teachers whose trails are reported above make specific reference to the need for staff development in approaches to problem-solving. The outcomes were very positive, with other teachers either using existing trails or producing their own. In order to stimulate such interest it will be necessary to show that maths trails are an effective means of teaching and assessing, of developing problem-solving strategies and skills.

Display of the children's work, both on the day of the trail, with photographs of the event, and subsequent work back in the class-room, will show the quality of the children's achievements. The outcomes are likely to be a mixture of written recording of the trail, the data collected and its interpretation. Further work back in school is likely to include models which children have made, math-ematical investigations which have been stimulated by something in the trail, and real-life mathematical problems for which children have found solutions. It is likely that cross-curricular aspects of the topics covered will have been developed, perhaps to include a scientific investigation, a model which uses the children's tech-nological skills, writing about what was seen and poems. All of this will give positive messages to other teachers of the effectiveness of trails as a means of working.

It is possible to develop maths trails which encourage more open-ended problem-solving. An example of this comes from a maths trail developed by a school in the south of England. Outside the school was a slabbed courtyard. The children were asked to find the shortest route from a slab at one end to a slab in the diagonally opposite corner, without jumping over any or crossing diagonally. The children needed to make decisions about the strategies they would use to solve this. It could be extended by a change of rules, or through setting each other pathway tasks, perhaps drawn on squared paper.

However, for the successful adoption of new teaching styles there needs to be a coherent plan for development. This is dis-cussed in Chapter 6.

Involvement of parents

Maths trails will often involve parents, who will accompany groups of children. This offers excellent opportunities to involve parents in their children's mathematics and for parents to see that 'doing' mathematics is not about producing pages of correct sums, but about children developing strategies and skills in their mathematics, where children use knowledge and understanding of how the number system operates, of pattern in algebra, of shape and space and so on. As Brissenden (1988) states, what is desirable is to have the active cooperation of parents in their children's learning of mathematics.

Displays of the children's work would encourage parents who saw it to appreciate the benefits for their children in this way of working. A parents' evening could be an opportunity for parents to try a maths trail for themselves; one which used the school environment would also enable parents to try some of the mathematical resources which their children use on a daily basis, thus promoting practical, exploratory activity from which generalizations can be made.

If parents have experienced maths trails for themselves, and have seen the benefits for their children's learning, then it is worth considering asking families to contribute ideas for further maths trails in the locality of the school. In some areas schools have produced books of favourite family recipes; it is suggested that favourite family trails could be used in a similar way.

Involvement of other schools

Winteridge (1989) suggests that schools in the locality could collaborate to devise maths trails for different abilities and age groups. Where schools have links with another school in a different location, for example inner-city with rural school, then it would be possible to organize visits to each other for the purpose of using already-devised trails in the locality.

Conclusion

The three teachers who described their experiences with maths trails showed that there were strong advantages in using this way of working, including the high level of achievement and satisfaction with their work by the children. There were issues which needed to be addressed if the use of trails was to be successful: careful planning; identification of a suitable trail location; planned preparation, including ancillary help; parental involvement, opportunities for staff development; and the possibilities of forming links with other schools to share trails. Maths trails do, as Salinger and Baker (1991) state, offer the opportunity to 'introduce children to the wonder of mathematics'. Maths trials offer the opportunity for children to see the world around them through 'mathematical' eyes and to appreciate the aesthetic beauty and the power of mathematics.

CHAPTER 3

Logo. Some Case Studies of Implementation in the Classroom

Some primary schools introduced Logo into their curriculum in the early 1980s, at a time when the British government provided funds to enable every primary school to purchase a half-price computer. Most of the primary educational software available in the early 1980s was of the drill and practice type, which produced 'sums' on the screen for children to fill in the correct answer. Logo offered the opportunity for children to write their own computer programs. Logo uses turtle graphics which allow children to program the turtle and to leave a trail, so that they can produce drawings on screen or on the floor if a floor turtle is used. Interesting early case studies can be found reported in Kelly (1984) and Hughes (1986).

The value of Logo is in the type of thinking which children need to use when solving a problem using it. In a typical classroom setting, the children will either have set themselves a problem or been set one by their teacher or another child. In order to solve the problem the children must make a plan, which allows them to break the problem down into a series of turtle moves, or computer commands. The shape which they want to build needs to be broken down into a series of moves by the turtle on the floor or the screen.

The use of Logo requires children to think in terms of movement by distance and turning through angle. It involves calculation, in order to produce the size of move required, and ordered or logical thinking, so that the drawing product is what is required. There is a translation between the shape to be produced and the means of producing it: the use of Logo language. It involves the use of problem-solving skills as children will need to form a plan, carry out their planning and evaluate the end result, and then to re-plan or modify the plan if the resultant drawing does not fulfil its purpose. Perhaps one of the most powerful arguments for the use of Logo in primary classrooms is that the children control the computer, rather than being controlled by it, as they program the turtle to create their chosen drawing.

Since the early 1980s programmable toys such as PIP and Roamer have been produced, both of which can be used to introduce early Logo language. Their advantage over screen-based Logo is that they move on the classroom floor, thus allowing children to interact with them within that environment, so that distances and angles are related to the classroom. Both PIP and Roamer can be programmed to move a reasonable distance for a FORWARD 1 command so that children can use small numbers in order to move the toy. Screen-based Logo requires the use of larger numbers in order to move the turtle a measurable distance. Teachers have found that their children relate positively to these programmable toys and then move to using screen-based Logo.

Both the 1989 and 1991 National Curriculum Mathematics make specific reference to Logo in the examples attached to the Statutory Orders (see Ma ATs 1/4a; 3/3b and 4c; 4/1b, 2b and 4b). Although the examples do not have the force of law, many schools decided to introduce Logo into their mathematics teaching. This chapter considers four case studies of the introduction of Logo, how this was planned, implemented and what the outcomes were. These are:

1. The use of a programmable toy in the reception class.
2. A developmental programme for children aged 5 to 7 years, using Logo with a concept keyboard and a floor turtle, and progressing to screen-based Logo.
3. The introduction of Logo to a Year 5 class (entry year) in a 9 to 13 middle school.
4. The use of Logo with a Year 6 class by an advisory teacher.

CASE STUDY

1. The use of a programmable toy in the reception class, contributed by Wendy Proctor

Wendy was the reception class teacher at a first school of approximately 200 children. She became interested in using IT in her classroom as part of an integrated curriculum, whilst studying for an INSET Early Childhood award. The children at the school were

47

drawn from a three-mile radius of the village, which was situated in a prosperous fruit and vegetable growing area. The school gave high priority to using cross-curricular themes in curriculum planning. The following account was written by her. Whilst Wendy's class used PIP, it should be noted that similar work can be done with the Valiant Roamer. Wendy refers to the 'times ten adaptor', which is a device which multiplies all numerical inputs into PIP by ten. This means that Forward 1, which normally involves a move of 1cm, becomes a move of 10cm. Turn Left 9, which normally means a turn to the left of 9°, becomes a turn to the left of 90°.

PIP stands for Programmable Interactive Plaything. It is a box shape with an on-board computer. There are 14 command buttons on the top operated by touch pads and it runs on battery power. A small attachment, which I called the 'times ten adaptor', enables the PIP to move in 10cm steps. The command keys are:

Numerals 0 to 9
TEST button
GO
Pause
END
Repeat
Clear entry (C.E.)
Clear Memory (C.M.)
Restore Memory (R.M.)
Arrow keys facing Forward, Backward, Left, Right

There is also the facility for a flashing light and to programme the PIP to play musical tunes.

I found that cardboard or construction toys such as Lego can be attached to PIP. PIP was presented as a 'mouse' with his own home layout plan which we made to place on the floor. The children insisted that PIP needed a friend so a cardboard 'friend' was made, whom the children named Arthur.

I began by involving the children in directional activities in PE. They imagined that they were PIP robots and made up short movement sequences such as 2 steps forward, 2 steps back, turn right, turn left. The use of this control toy was an introduction to Logo which will be used by the children later in school. The children experimented in using PIP. When I sat with groups I directed the activities towards mathematical concepts. Without my input the children concentrated on PIP finding Arthur in a play activity. The emphasis was on the children using PIP in an experimental play situation. The command buttons used most frequently were: numbers, direction, light flash, clear memory, TEST, GO. A simple instruction given by the children was: Clear Memory, Forwards 3, Turn Right, Go.

Wendy introduced her class to simple action and movement songs which involved the children in following instructions for moving. They particularly enjoyed the Hokey Cokey, which encouraged left and right movements. On the floor of the classroom Wendy stuck coloured tape in the form of a cross. The children were encouraged, one at a time, to follow instructions walking along the tape, to take 5 steps forward, to turn left or right, then to move forwards or backwards. This was done to ensure that they all understood the commands which were needed to move PIP as the language used followed the same language patterns which would be used with Logo.

Activities with PIP not only practised fine-motor coordination skills, but mathematical and geographical skills too. The children counted and coded-in how many steps PIP took to a certain position and there was the beginning of addition and subtraction, when the children had to take an extra step or go back as too many steps had been taken. I made this computation more practical by making a set of card 'mouse' feet, each 10cm long, so that the children could set them out on the floor to show PIP's progress along the chosen route. I felt that the children were too young to understand the significance of 90 degrees in a corner but, using the 'times ten adaptor', they could code-in 9 after a turn input; I referred to 9 as a 'magic number for turning a corner'. I am sure that this will be of value later. With my support, the children began to sequence instructions for PIP, trying to combine more than one command. The children were actively engaged in their tasks.

The beginnings of this programme of work involved the children in understanding the language of movement; Wendy used PE as an opportunity to develop this language. In order that the children can use PIP effectively they need to know and understand the following commands.

Forward, Backward: go on or back; move on or back, run, walk, etc: reception and Year 1 children are likely already to associate this language with their own movements and the direction in which they are moving.

Right, Left: implies direction of turn. This is much more difficult for young children, who will understand the need for turning but not discriminate between right and left directions. Nor do young children differentiate by name between their left and right hands or feet – reception class children will put their shoes on the wrong feet. Wendy tried putting coloured bands on children's arms to help them to distinguish left from right; this was successful.

Numerals 0 to 9 as measure of quantity: the children had had experience of using numerals to define nominal and cardinal number.

Go and End: these imply starting and stopping and were already understood.

Pause, Repeat, Clear Memory, Clear Entry: the children learnt what these meant as they became familiar with programming PIP.

PE activities where children follow instructions for moving can help children to develop their understanding for this language, for example: five steps forward, turn right , three steps forward. These instructions can become more complex as the children's understanding grows. The children can play games where they give each other instructions. For instance, large paper arrows can be made and set out in a pattern on the floor of the hall; a child can follow the directions that other children give him or her in order to follow the arrows. Similarly, chalked lines or masking tape lines can be placed on the hall floor and children can give each other instructions for following these. Such games can mimic Logo in that the children can take control of 'programming' each other, can make a plan and test it out.

These activities are designed to develop the use and understanding of the language patterns associated with Logo. In order to facilitate the progression from the children's own movements and associated language, floor-based turtle Logo and screen-based Logo, it is suggested that the teacher should encourage the children to use the Logo language forms in order to describe their own movements and that of, say, PIP or Roamer. The example given above (five steps forward, turn right, three steps forward, in BBC version Logo, becomes FORWARD 5 RIGHT FORWARD 3. In this way the formal Logo language can be internalized by the children. As children move to using a floor-based turtle, it is necessary to input a value for the turn. With PIP it is possible to use an adaptor which turns an input of 9 units into an input of 90 degrees; with Roamer it is possible to re-programme the value of the units used.

The children in Wendy's class were told what to input when using PIP in order to turn through a right angle. Wendy referred to 9, the input for a right-angled turn, as 'a magic number for turning a corner.' The investigative work which the children carried out involved distance rather than angle.

Counting and measuring can be developed, as in Wendy's use of 'mouse feet' for identifying how many PIP had to move in order to reach his chosen goal. This offers children experience in measuring with non-standard units. In this case the mouse feet were 10cm long, which represented 1 unit of movement length for PIP, when using the adaptor. Children can estimate how far, set out the mouse feet to see how far, and check by inputting an appropriate amount and pressing GO.

Estimation is a life skill which we all need to develop. For example, about how far is it to the end of the road? How fast is that car going? How long will it take me to walk to the shops? About how much electrical wire do I need to complete a wiring job? How much does this parcel weigh? Which holds more, this jug or that one? It is important that children recognize that an estimate does not represent a right or wrong answer, but is an informed judgement. The ability to make a reasonably accurate judgement improves when children (and adults) have the opportunity to compare their estimate with their measure.

The language associated with measurement can be developed through PIP/Logo activities. Measurement is approximate, and is only as accurate as the tools used and the person using them. In Wendy's classroom, the mouse feet were used as a guide to the size of the numerical input needed to move PIP; sometimes the feet showed that there was a bit more or less in the measure than their estimate, and these experiences led to the understanding of the need for greater accuracy and for standard units in measuring.

In order to move PIP around his house layout, the children started by moving PIP by 1 or 2 units until they had moved him to the room where Arthur, his friend, waited. Wendy encouraged them to repeat this by finding how many mouse feet lengths PIP had moved altogether to get to the chosen room then to try inputting that. So, for example:

    FORWARD 1   FORWARD 2   FORWARD 1
became
    FORWARD 4

This was the beginning of the children's work on addition and subtraction, without using either the language associated with computation or the symbols. The practical experience involved combining amounts of 'mouse feet' and the children began to develop mental strategies for doing this.

Wendy introduced combinations of commands. The children found that PIP could be made to turn and to move forward or back, using just one series of commands. She noted the conversation between two children:

Adam:	Let's make him (PIP) go over there to the cupboard.
Barry:	I'll make him go. (He pressed Forward 3 (30cm) then Right 9. GO.)
Barry:	Oh no, he's gone the wrong way.
Adam:	I'll have him back now. (He pressed Back 2, Right 9, GO.)
	(PIP travelled much further than was expected.)
Barry:	Did you make him do all that?
Adam:	No. I forgot to Clear Memory. Silly me. Let me do it again.

The experience of 'de-bugging' a program is helpful as the identification of the error(s) can become the new starting point for further investigation; de-bugging is seen as an important part of developing problem-solving strategies by Senior (1989) and Underwood and Underwood (1990). Adam saw that PIP had not done what he expected: his reasoning, that PIP had in fact completed both sets of instructions because Clear Memory had not been used, was correct. By the end of the project PIP could be programmed by the children to enter his house, move to a room, turn and go into the room to meet Arthur, all of which could be done in one sequence of commands.

In a similar project in another school, a different approach was adopted. The project began when the children were about 5 years old. The children used a floor turtle which was attached to the computer by a wire and could be operated from either the computer keyboard or through a concept keyboard. This account is based upon detailed discussions between the teachers concerned and the author, and on classroom observation of the children using Logo in the term following the completion of the project. It should be noted that in the following three case studies Logotron Logo was used.

CASE STUDY

2. A developmental programme for children aged 5 to 7 years, using Logo with a concept keyboard and floor turtle, and progressing to screen-base Logo, with a contribution from Denise A.

The primary school was situated in an urban area within two miles of the centre of a Midlands city. There were approximately 400 children aged 3 to 11 on roll. The local population was mainly Asian, with some Arab, Afro-Caribbean and white families. The mathematics coordinator, Denise, had taught at the school for 17 years. At the time of this interview she was about to leave to go to another school within the borough, a side-ways move to a head of

52

infants post. Denise had been involved, with other Early Years teachers in the school, in the PLUM project: Primary Logo Users in Mathematics; she was the project coordinator within the school. The school had been one of those chosen because Denise had, the previous year, attended a mathematics inservice course, on which the project leader for the LEA had taught and had got to know her quite well.

The project was set up to run for two terms in Year 1 and two terms in Year 2, to monitor the children's mathematical progress through the use of Logo. The project leader offered support to me and the other teachers involved at the school, by working alongside us for half a day every fortnight. We had parallel Year 1 classes at the start of the project.

The majority of the children in our classes spoke English as a second language. Some of the children were reasonably fluent in English, whilst others, at the start of the project, were not. We began by planning activities in PE which involved direction and movement. The children played robot games, first following our instructions and then by working in pairs, giving each other instructions to follow. The language which was used for the instructions was based upon Logo commands, so that the children learnt the commands and what they meant by using them to move themselves. We saw this as imperative: the children would need to understand the Logo commands when they used the floor-based turtle and later, when using screen-based Logo.

Once the commands were understood the children worked in groups of four with a floor turtle. This was controlled by the computer so that the children needed to be aware of the trailing wire. Within their groups of four, one child was responsible for inputting commands through the concept keyboard, another decided what the commands should be, a third held the wire to the turtle, to keep it out of harm and the fourth observed. The children changed these jobs around between them so that all of them experienced each role. The initial use of the concept keyboard enabled the children to identify a command on the overlay and to input that without needing to type the command in at the keyboard.

A 'turtle village' had been built by the children which included buildings and streets which the turtle could be programmed to navigate. The teaching and learning experiences from this were cross-curricular, including technology, art, mathematics and science in the village's construction and writing stories about the village. The children decorated the village housing with repeating patterns just as shop fronts in the local high street have been decorated with ethnic patterns by their Asian owners.

As in Wendy's classroom, there was an emphasis upon the children being able to understand and use the language of Logo. For many of the children in Denise's and the other teachers' classes this was their introduction to these language patterns in English. The first main issue which arose was that of big numbers.

Traditionally, whichever published scheme you use, Year 1 children 'do' numbers up to 10 and Year 2 children 'do' numbers up to 20. In using Logo in this way, teachers are asking the same children to conceptualize much larger numbers than would traditionally have been introduced.

In order to give the children a wide range of experience of larger numbers, we used house numbers, number lines, 100 squares, calculator games. By the beginning of Year 2, many of the children were confident with large numbers, could order them, and had developed knowledge and understanding of how the place value system worked. All the schools involved in the project reported the same finding.

The children worked with a range of numbers that was outside the teachers' experience of what children had normally achieved in Year 1. The importance of involving the children in using these numbers, in searching for pattern was seen by all schools involved in the PLUM project. Similar findings have been identified through the PrIME Project (Shuard *et al.*, 1991), where children used calculators as part of their mathematics work. The children in Denise's class enjoyed working with larger numbers, knew the names of these numbers and had experience of them in life outside school, through house numbers, bus and car numbers, telephone numbers and so on (this is discussed in more detail in Chapter 4). Children were involved in using addition in order to move the turtle through the street in the village they had built.

To move the screen turtle from Home to a required point will involve using large numbers as a Logo move of 1 unit is a tiny amount. Children will input forward commands until they have moved the turtle to the chosen place. This could be:

FORWARD 10   FORWARD 10   FORWARD 10

which would produce a move of 30 units. However, Denise found that by developing mental methods of calculation, by investigating number patterns and through experience in using calculators as an aid, many of the children became adept at using larger numbers in order to identify a turtle move.

The development of the concept of angle was continued from PE activities involving the children giving and receiving instructions to turn themselves, with work involving clock faces and angles of turn. The children explored moving the big hand on the clock face from 12 to 3, using Logo. By trial and error they found that they needed an input of 90 degrees. From this they tried moving the hand from 12 to 6 and again by trial and error found that an input of 180 degrees was required. Dilshad, a 6-year-old child in Year 2, wanted to work out what angle of turn he would need to move the clock hand from 12 to 9. He knew that this involved three lots of 90:

90 is nearly a hundred and three lots of a hundred is 300 and I've got to take some off.

He gave the correct answer, using mental calculations. We observed that the children devised their own methods of calculation, using mainly mental methods.

With the experience of using large numbers and of investigating number patterns, Dilshad had developed his own method of calculating. He saw a pattern which he could use (hundreds) in order to find 3 x 90. Papert (1981) wrote: '…children are the active builders of their own intellectual structures'. Dilshad had used his understanding of how one part of the number system operated in order to produce a method for multiplying with another. This was an important development for him: he had developed strategies which allowed him to identify the problem and to seek solutions.

During the second term of the project, some of the children were ready to be taught how to use a repeat command, combining two inputs, in order to draw a regular shape. Mikhail used:

Repeat 4 (FD 100 RT 90)

and drew a square. By the end of the project, some of the children were able to define their own procedures and to use these within other procedures in order to produce quite complex shapes. The children were not expected to remember commands: once a new command or procedure had been introduced we wrote it on a large strip of card. These were kept by the computer in the classroom so that they were there for the children to use as required.

By using cards with commands and procedures the children had quickly gained the confidence to find the procedure they required and to incorporate it into their work. These cards belonged to the children; their teacher had written them out for them as they learnt new procedures but they were stacked by the computer and the children had free access to them. There was no labelling of the commands or procedures – the children were able to pick out the one that was needed by reading it and understanding what it meant.

The project finished at the end of the spring term of Year 2. During the summer term, four children in my class continued to work on every possible occasion at the computer, using Logo. They were able to load Logo from the disc onto the A3000, produce squares, triangles, rectangles, circles and combinations of these to make recognizable pictures. By trial and error they would produce any polygon and enjoyed being set a challenge. One child was particularly interested in producing random line patterns, using the WRAP command. This group of children consisted of three boys and one girl. Chris spoke English at home, Satwinder and Andip spoke Urdu, Kulvinder spoke Gujerati. Their chosen language at the computer was always English, which ensured that Chris was never excluded, even though at other times in the classroom, both Gujerati and Urdu were frequently used. These four children were the main users of the computer in the classroom; this, on occasions, caused tension between them and other groups who wanted an opportunity to use Logo.

We found that some of the children, by the end of Year 2, were working at level 4 in Mathematics for some aspects of shape and space and number, and levels 4 and 5 in technology (IT strand). I believe that the Logo experience has motivated the children in all their mathematics work, as they had generally achieved more in mathematics by the end of Year 2 than previously. The other teacher and I find that our own level of confidence with using IT in our mathematics teaching is much higher.

Underwood and Underwood (1990) point to evidence which confirms that young children who have undergone a programme of work with Logo have demonstrated improved understanding in number and shape concepts. The evidence from Denise's class would support this. What was also noted, by both Wendy and Denise, was the improvement in the children's understanding and use of mathematical vocabulary. Children were actively involved in discussions with each other, planning their work, discussing outcomes and forming revised plans. They had learned about larger numbers, explored ways of calculating with them and had developed their own methods of calculation. The excitement for Denise and her colleagues lay in the children's demonstration of what they had achieved: mastery and control of the use of larger numbers, the power of their thinking which had led them to further discoveries and which gave them ownership of their learning and understanding. Above all, the enthusiasm for this way of working, with the children being allowed to take control of their learning and to make decisions about ways forward, was seen as a major achievement by the teachers. My discussions with the children showed how enthusiastic they were to continue this work.

I am concerned that the children are unlikely to receive any further Logo experience when they move to the junior part of the school in September, as there is no member of staff with either the interest or the expertise to continue the work. My post as mathematics coordinator will not be filled until the following January. Of the other teachers involved with me in the PLUM project, one is about to take maternity leave and the other has been given the English coordinator's role and would be fully occupied with that. It seems unlikely that the work of the project will continue.

One other teacher had expressed interest in getting started with Logo. There had been one planned staff development session for Logo during the lifetime of the project. The school was well-resourced for computer hardware, but this tended to be used for either word-processing or for drill-and-practice-type programs. When asked about computer awareness, most of the staff expressed concern at their limited skills.

> I started the project feeling that I knew nothing about the use of IT in the classroom. I had had to have an instruction sheet to remind me where to plug the turtle in and how to attach the concept keyboard. After four terms of working with Logo I am now confident in the use of the hardware, and am determined to continue to use Logo in my new post. At the start of the project, one of the other teachers would not touch the computer for fear that she would damage it. By the end of the project she used IT for Logo and for desktop publishing with her class of Year 1 children and felt much more confident in teaching mathematics.

The children involved in the PLUM project had enjoyed a much richer mathematical curriculum than was usual at this school. They had:

- used large numbers in their classroom activities, traditionally the reserve of the junior department;
- used combinations of pencil and paper, mental methods and calculators in computation;
- understood about angle of turn and were able to use angle in order to produce complex shapes;
- could use procedures to produce shapes and thus had some insights into the meanings of algebraic notation, such as the use of brackets within operations;
- had developed skills of identifying a problem, of using trial and error processes to find solutions;
- were actively using their mathematical knowledge and understanding to solve problems;
- had acquired personal qualities of collaboration, independence and perseverance;
- could talk about their mathematics to raise questions and discuss with their peers and teacher for planning and recall purposes.

It is interesting to compare the progress made by Denise's class with that made by children in their first year at middle school. The following was written by the class teacher.

CASE STUDY

3. The introduction of Logo to a Year 5 class, by John Birchley

I taught a Year 5 class, the intake year of a 9 to 13 middle school. Liaison with contributory first schools was good, but there was that inevitable disjointedness between Y4 and Y5 that goes with transfer from one school to another. Within this class the children transferred from four first schools and they had received different experiences in all areas of the curriculum even though there was agreement on many curriculum issues within the pyramid of schools. I found that my pupils had had limited experience with computers and none of them had used Logo before.

During a Mathematics INSET course I had worked with other course members to produce a booklet for ourselves entitled, 'All you ever wanted to know about Logo, but dared not ask'. This was intended to be used in schools, but was also a response to some course members' feelings of inadequacy about using Logo in the classroom. I chose to use this booklet and other Logo resources which were already in school as my starting point for introducing my class to Logo.

In my school there is a computer room, which contains 12 computers, a mix of BBC B, Master Compacts and A3000s; I also have a Master Compact in my classroom. Each Y5 class is timetabled for a 50-minute lesson each week in the computer room; this is for familiarization with the rudiments of computer use, learning how to turn it on, load a disc, load a program, etc. and then using a series of programs to familiarize themselves with the computer and, particularly, the keyboard. The activities that I was to plan would need to fit in to this one lesson a week format as the computer room was fully booked at all other times and the one computer in my classroom was already heavily utilized for other purposes. I decided to produce a series of tasks for the children to attempt, rather than prepare a series of lessons to be taught. I wanted to give my children the opportunity to learn through discovery and experience rather than just teaching them the procedures to follow.

The tasks, after an initial class lesson introduction, were produced as single sheet worksheets, in order that individuals or pairs could discuss and progress at an appropriate pace. This allowed for the teacher to be present at some stages, but also to be able to leave pupils to their own discoveries when I was dealing with other groups.

My intentions were to:

1. encourage pupils with no previous experience of Logo (or of floor-based turtles) to use it;
2. familiarize pupils with the program commands, abbreviations and what they would produce on screen;
3. allow pupils to work independently when necessary;
4. promote discussion;
5. use open-ended tasks, rather than closed, where possible.

The first lesson took place in the school's computer room, during their third term. I told the children that I wanted to show them something different.

I deliberately located myself as far away from the computer with Logo already loaded as I could and stood looking lost until a pupil asked me what was wrong. I told them that I wanted to get to 'that computer over there' but was not sure of the best way to do it. Soon a number of different ways were suggested.

A volunteer was found to direct me. As each instruction was given I followed it literally, walking into walls and climbing over desks. Very soon, with the help of the other pupils, the commands became more sophisticated. I was told how many paces to take, forwards, backwards, how much to turn to the left or right. Eventually they chose a clock face type of instruction for this. Finally I arrived at my chosen computer.

Seated at the computer I told the class that the computer was a turtle who would do exactly what it was told if the instructions were correct. First, how to make the turtle appear on the screen: eventually the correct command of 'show turtle' was suggested. What about moving around the screen? Forward, Go forward, Straight ahead, were suggested but with no results. Eventually, the need for a unit attached to the command was suggested. Soon, Show turtle, Hide turtle, Forward n, (where n is a numerical input), Back n, Right n and Left n were all being used successfully.

The abbreviated commands were introduced next. The full version took a long time to type. Using these we drew a square, a procedure with four separate commands. There was as yet no realization of the units being used in commands, just an awareness that the larger the number the further the turtle moved. Degrees and angles were not discussed; these were simply numbers at this stage.

The second session gave the pupils hands-on experience of using Logo. They familiarized themselves with the use of the abbreviated commands and what they produced on the screen. All the pupils managed the following commands:

Show Turtle	ST
Hide Turtle	HT
Forward	FD
Back	BK
Left	LT
Right	RT
Home	H
Clean	CLEAN
Clear Screen	CS

From here, pupils used turtle pathway worksheets which encouraged investigation of size and direction of moves around the screen by the turtle. These produced much discussion about how much to turn and how far to go. Another sheet proved to be more problematic. It shows the map of a river with some bridges across. The turtle thinks, 'I wonder if I can walk across each bridge only once and finish where I started'. The answer is no, it cannot be done. Pupils expected to be able to complete the task and became frustrated. Much discussion was involved and then the pupils tried to complete the task with one 'double-cross' which proved possible.

A strong argument for the use of Logo in classrooms put forward by Papert (see Reid and Rushton, 1985) was that children should not feel constrained by the 'only one correct answer' syndrome and that they should move to searching for a range of solutions to a problem. The difficulty with the above problem for John's children was two-fold. First, the question was closed. Second, the answer was 'no', one that perhaps children do not meet very often in school.

Once pupils had succeeded in drawing a square, I taught the Repeat command and demonstrated it for a square. Pupils were asked to use the Repeat to produce an equilateral triangle. This proved problematic. Pupils asked the turtle to run through angles of 60 degrees. After much discussion most pupils understood that the turtle turned on the external angle of the triangle and that an input of 120 degrees was required.

The next task was to produce a copy on screen of a drawing of a building. This involved using the commands Pen up, Pen down, Wipe, Clear Screen.

The next set of tasks asked pupils to read a set of Logo commands then to visualize the results and to draw them before trying the commands on screen. Some of the units of length were very small. One child commented: 'Can I times those by 10 or you'll never see them'. For example:

FORWARD 40
LEFT 120
FORWARD 40
LEFT 120
FORWARD 40
LEFT 120

would produce a very small equilateral triangle.

Towards the end of the term, some pupils had finished all the tasks which I produced. They moved on to self-initiated tasks. One very popular one was to investigate the Repeat command by seeing how large a number the computer would repeat and then sit and watch it do so. Changing the screen and turtle's colour was also popular, but pupils were disappointed when printing as this was in monochrome.

The opportunity to plan their own tasks opened up new opportunities for the children. The children took control of their work and the Logo language when freed from the teacher-driven task. Testing variables through using colour or the Repeat command allowed the children to form hypotheses and to test these. At this point, when they initiated their own tasks, the children had taken control of their own learning.

Pupils, who had no previous experience of using Logo, were quickly able to use the program, commands and abbreviations, enjoyed the work and valued their results. The nature of the tasks planned and the production of these as single worksheets facilitated the pupils working independently. This was necessary as pupils worked at different rates and with different levels of understanding.

As an introduction to Logo, the worksheet approach was useful. However, I do feel that pupils of this age could do so much more with Logo than I attempted in this project. For the future, I would like to be able to integrate Logo with the shape and angle work normally undertaken in Year 5. For this year, Logo was studied in isolation from the rest of the mathematics curriculum and this lessened its effectiveness as it was more difficult for pupils to make the connections with their current knowledge and understanding. In future, tasks should be more demanding of the pupils and be linked with other areas of mathematics. I would like to have the opportunity of more than one lesson a week. This would mean a change in policy for access to the computer room.

In his evaluation of his class's work, John shows how much he learnt through using Logo: he acknowledges the importance of the relevance to the children of what they are asked to do; the Logo work was undertaken in isolation from the rest of the curriculum; he is aware that the children can do more than was asked of them, which became apparent particularly when they were free to set their own tasks. They set challenges which had meaning to them, which allowed them to explore variables and to test hypotheses. John's realization that he can improve on this work, that he can extend and enrich the learning for the children, will encourage him to request the changes in school policy which are needed in order to allow for more effective access to computers.

On a recent visit to feeder first schools I found that a great deal more work with Logo had been covered. Schools use Roamer, PIP and screen-based Logo. We plan to purchase a Roamer for school. For the next cohort of pupils entering school this would mean that Logo work would already have begun and thus I would hope to achieve far more than has been possible this year. I would hope to facilitate improvement in pupils' use of mathematical language and vocabulary and their expression of their own ideas.

For some of Denise's Year 2 children, the introduction of variables could have been the next stage. The four main users of Logo in her classroom could already use simple procedures which they defined for themselves, then saved and used within new procedures. The introduction of a variable, where the procedure, for example, for squares, could be used to generate a range of squares, to make patterns, to investigate star patterns made from sequences of squares, might have formed the next stage of learning. The use of variables is discussed in the next case study.

CASE STUDY

4. The use of Logo with a Year 6 class, contributed by Paul Broadbent

The following came from an interview with Paul, an advisory teacher for information technology, with a particular interest in mathematics. As an advisory teacher Paul had the opportunity to work with a Year 6 class. The children started with making spirals on paper and became interested in generating spirals using Logo. In the illustrations for this section, the term SLOWDUMP refers to the print command for this version of Logo.

Interviewer: How did you organize this?

Paul: We started with a large sheet of squared paper with a group of children working around that. We generated a spiral from two numbers. Because it was squared paper it was always a 90 degree turn. We had been doing a lot of work on rule-making. They were used to working in an investigative way and were used to setting themselves rules.

Interviewer: What rules did you set?

Paul: We made the rule: it's going to be a 90 degree turn. We made the rule that the turn was always to be in the same direction. The line lengths were also set, like 5 then 6, 5 then 6. This made a rectangle so the children investigated adding a third number to make the spiral, like 5, 6, 7. This made a closed spiral. I just literally showed them one spiral like that and said, 'What can we find, what does a 3, 4 look like or a 1, 2' and set them off to investigate the different spirals produced by using different combinations. What they were good at was setting themselves questions like 'Let's find out this'.

Interviewer: And Logo?

Paul: A group of the children had come across Logo; they hadn't done a lot. They could see that this generating spirals could work really well using Logo. So the group wanted to use that. To begin with they did it by setting up a procedure called SPIRAL and physically writing it all out, and it (the computer) would do it. That was fine and they spent a couple of days on it. But it was a bit of a bore.

```
?REPEAT 4 [FD 100 RT 90 FD 130 RT 90 FD
160 RT 90]
?SLOWDUMP
```

Figure 3.1 Procedure for drawing a spiral

Interviewer: What records did they keep?

Paul: They printed it out and stuck the print-out on some paper and then wrote about what they'd found. That took them a long while because they had produced a different procedure for every different spiral. I didn't want to go on to using variables but they actually said that this was getting a bit laborious. So I had to teach procedures using variables and they took to it really easily.

Interviewer: What was the variable?

Paul: We stuck to RIGHT 90 so the only variable was the side. We used:

TO SPIRAL :A :B :C
REPEAT 4[FD :A RT 90 FD :B RT 90 FD :C RT 90]
END

Then the children decided upon values for A, B, C and entered the command, say, SPIRAL 120, 150, 180.

```
?TO SPIRAL :A :B :C
>REPEAT 4[FD :A RT 90 FD :B RT 90 FD :
RT 90]
>END
SPIRAL DEFINED
?SPIRAL 120 150 180
?SLOWDUMP
```

Figure 3.2 Procedure for drawing a spiral, where the distances are variable

So, from then on it was really easy: SPIRAL 60 80 100; SPIRAL 100 150 200; and so on

Interviewer: So then they were re-doing what they had already investigated.

Paul: Yes, but doing it so much quicker. And also they could generate new ones. They started to ask other questions about the area of the square which these spirals fit inside. They wanted to know if there was a relationship between the two numbers and the square within which the spiral fitted. And they found that there was. They found an algebraic relationship, not a difficult one. It was a great discovery. Exciting stuff!

Interviewer: What do you feel were the advantages of this type of investigative work, using Logo?

Paul: There was that sort of investigation, which pushed the children on to look at algebraic relationships. But there were some children who took this on further. They said, 'If I can change the length variable I could also change the angle'. They'd only used 90 degrees so far, which produced neat, closed spirals. So we then moved on to SPIRAL 2, which was a different procedure, with

REPEAT 4 [FORWARD :A RIGHT :D FORWARD :B RIGHT :D FORWARD :C RIGHT :D]

and then you had to put in, say, 100 120 140 75, where 75 is the angle of turn.

```
?TO SPIRAL2 :A :B :C :D
>REPEAT 4 [FD :A RT :D FD :B RT :D FD :C
 RT :D]
>END
SPIRAL2 DEFINED
?SPIRAL2 100 120 140 75
?SLOWDUMP
```

Figure 3.3 Procedure for drawing a spiral, where the distances and angles are variable

Interviewer: Did the children find this difficult?

Paul: No. It's not terribly complicated. It's just understanding the meaning of the Logo language, which the children found easy to manage as they used their previous experience with it. They were trying to predict what their input variables would produce. And obviously, with the change of angle, they then opened it out, not so much as a maths investigation, although they could then start predicting whether it was an open or closed spiral, but not so much numerical work, they weren't using algebraic formulae. They produced some wonderful designs and patterns. These looked really impressive when printed out on paper as well. That way, the children felt that they had done something, achieved something, generated all this in a simple way, really.

Interviewer: How do you view the use of Logo?

Paul: The best work, really, I've seen with Logo has been the shape investigations. You know, design a tent with it, design a house. I've seen some lovely work.

The first activity, with a group of children working with their teacher, Paul, on a large sheet of squared paper, offered a practical way into the investigation of generating spirals. The extension into using Logo offered opportunities for the children to investigate further, using their knowledge and understanding of shape and space, measures, number and algebra. They could predict which inputs would produce a closed or open spiral, they understood that the lengths of the sides would determine the area of the resultant square and they could use variables within algebraic sentences. These children were already used to working in an investigative way; that was not new. They brought to the Logo activity existing knowledge and understanding which they had the confidence to use in order to extend their knowledge through further investigation.

Benefits of using Logo

All the children involved in these four studies were reported by their teachers as having learned new mathematics concepts through the work with Logo. Logo language allowed all the children access to a mathematical language which enabled them to develop their understanding of concepts through the interlinking of different strands of knowledge and understanding. These strands became dependent upon each other. In Wendy's class, the children developed understanding of ordinal and cardinal number whilst measuring using 'mouse feet'. Denise's children had investigated angle of turn, which involved them in understanding and using large numbers and had led to the development of individual methods of calculation. In John's class there was the opportunity to develop the processes associated with investiga-tional methodology, for the children and John to discover the power of learning through child-initiated tasks. John intended to seize the opportunity to promote this work through the school.

The experiences of Wendy, Denise, John and Paul all led to an increase in their own confidence levels in using IT and to an en-riched curriculum for their children. Denise and her colleagues had used concept keyboards previously as an aid to the production of children's writing. The use of one for mathematical learning of-fered new possibilities. The children did not need to use the com-puter keyboard until they were ready to distinguish the keys in order to input words and numerals. The overlays had been set up to produce simple commands, which gave all the children access to Logo language. They were not reliant upon their reading ability, nor upon their ability to distinguish between letters on the keyboard in order to input commands to the turtle.

However, Denise's main concern centred around what would be done to continue this development when the children moved into the junior department of the school. Her fear was that this work would not be continued and that the benefit that the children had received from this project would be lost. This concern was shared by Wendy, who commented that once the children left the reception class the Logo work would not be continued. Paul, as advisory teacher, considered Logo work to be patchy, that one teacher in a school may be interested but that there was unlikely to be a follow-through within the school. John found that there was a growing interest in feeder first schools so that there would be opportunities for future developments. Similarly, the use of concept keyboards is limited. Many schools have one, still tucked away in a cupboard, or its use is confined to the reception class or for children with specific learning difficulties. It is suggested that the issues which confine the use of new technology in mathematics teaching are common to the introduction of all new forms of technology, not just to the use of Logo, concept keyboards or new software.

Denise and the project supervisor for PLUM produced a first draft of a short report for schools. It helped to clarify the stage of development that the teachers involved in the project had reached and was intended to help other schools to plan the introduction of Logo into their curriculum. Each of the points within the report has had comments added in order to consider the relevant factors which may influence decisions within schools. The report is reproduced below.

Influencing Colleagues
The bare necessities

1. Seriously you do not need to know much about Logo in order to start work and you can learn with the children. You shouldn't feel threatened or inadequate. It is helpful if you can work with a colleague who is sympathetic with what you are doing.

Feelings of inadequacy and insecurity amongst teachers with regard to using IT have been well-documented. Hughes (1986) refers to resistance amongst teachers to using Logo with young children. Working with another colleague offers opportunities to share successes and difficulties, to discuss ways of overcoming problems, to learn together; this removes the feeling of isolation.

The colleague does not have to work in the same school: it can be someone who is teaching the same age group so that it is possible to plan together and to compare notes on outcomes.

2. You must have support from the Senior Management Team if Logo is going to succeed.

Is there a curriculum consultant within the school for IT, for mathematics? They will be able to offer help and support. To use either Logo or concept keyboards will involve some cost to the school: computer printout paper, perhaps the purchase of new hardware. There will be INSET courses available for IT which it may be useful to attend, so the headteacher's support could include provision of course fees.

3. You will need a computer, monitor, printer, disk drive and Logo chip or disc to start work. This must be in place in your classroom for a reasonable length of time in order to establish your own confidence and competence as well as that of the children.

In order to make good use of the hardware it must be available on demand in the classroom. The implications for using both concept keyboards and Logo are that the possibilities for use will increase with experience. For the children to become proficient in using either, they will need a reasonable length of time to become familiar with each new step. Most classrooms now have their own computer; however, the use of both Logo and concept keyboard overlays will involve dedicating the hardware to this purpose in order that all the children within the class have the opportunity to use it. The implication could be that if screen-based Logo is used then either the computer station is dedicated to this purpose for the life of the project or another computer station is needed so that children still have access to other facilities such as word-processing, data processing, etc.

The children in Denise's class worked in groups of three or four at the computer station. Such was the level of their interest that each group would want at least an hour to plan, discuss, try out ideas, then to produce their finished piece of work, save it and print it out. On some occasions the work was saved for another session as they had not finished.

Both teachers operated a record system which checked that all children had access to the computer. In both cases the time spent on the project involved work with the hardware and work away from the computer. Straker (1989) identified that computer usage needs to be related to the children's own experiences. The interrelation between 'hands-on' and 'hands-off' time on particular activities enables the children to form links between activities and to move towards forming generalizations.

4. Get in touch with your Microtechnology Unit, where they are very helpful and knowledgeable regarding Logo.

Denise's LEA provided an excellent resource at the teachers' centre which was staffed by advisory teachers who offered inservice courses and support within classrooms. Wendy had similar support from her LEA.

5. Working with colleagues. You will need to prove that the work you are doing is valuable. Does it meet the National Curriculum Guidelines? We can advise you that it does and our experience shows that the use of Logo has a very positive effect upon the children's learning.

Logo is mentioned in the examples given for the 1991 revision of the National Curriculum Mathematics. It is used in examples for algebra and shape and space. The Non-Statutory Guidance contains references to children using Logo (section F3, paragraph 3.4). Section D1, using and applying mathematics, contains three broad strands: using mathematics; communicating in mathematics; developing ideas of argument and proof. Logo can be used as an agent of development for all of the objectives listed in these strands.

6. You need to gain the interest of your colleagues. You have to be seen to be doing the work yourself. It is often worthwhile taking the time to display children's work in a prominent position signifying its importance to staff, children and visitors to the school.

The support of other teachers in the school is vital if the work begun is to continue in other classrooms. However, the children also need to know that their efforts are valued. By displaying their work they can take pride in their achievements and for parents and other visitors to the school, this offers the chance to see what has been achieved.

7. Gaining the interest of your colleagues can be difficult due to curriculum demands but somehow you have to project your enthusiasm alongside the positive contribution that Logo can offer the children.

With the support of the senior management team within the school and of the LEA support service, a useful way of involving other staff members in the initiative can be to run an inservice session. This could involve some of the children who have taken part in the project, so that they can discuss their work with other teachers and show what they can do. Alternatively, if the head-teacher is willing to release teachers on a rota basis, then others can come to observe the children at work in the classroom. Other teachers will need evidence of the benefits of the project: it must be shown to be worth the time and effort that will need to be invested.

8. At some time you will need to look at continuity and progression throughout the school. Eventually it has to be developed into a whole school policy for it to be worthwhile in order to benefit the children.

If the project is to have maximum potential then there needs to be a clear policy statement which identifies the need for continuity and progression throughout the school. The stages of development for the children need to be clearly stated. If the extension of the project is to be effective then the resource issue will need to be considered.

A year after Wendy had completed her project with the reception children, her headteacher decided that the benefits for these children needed to be available for all children in the school. He enrolled in an inservice course for IT in order to improve his own knowledge and skill with IT; during this time the staff considered in detail what Wendy had achieved. It was decided to develop a whole-school policy for IT and to include with this a carefully costed resource development plan so that sufficient hardware to support this could be purchased from capitation and from fundraising. Wendy was closely involved in these developments. Her expertise was utilized throughout the school and she offered to run inservice sessions for staff. A newly appointed mathematics coordinator was also interested in using IT in mathematics and she proved to be another supporter of staff members who did not share this level of confidence.

9. Liaison with your High School is helpful. You can often show them the dizzy heights your children have reached. They have expertise that can be of use. It is important to show them that.

The need for liaison is not just between primary and secondary schools but also across other primary schools in the area. In some parts of Britain primary schools have formed clusters which share responsibilities for staff development. A new initiative in one school can lead to others in the locality sharing that experience and becoming part of a larger initiative. The high school can share in this, offering support and showing interest in what has been achieved. If the high school can identify how it will utilize the children's expertise when they transfer to high school, staff of the feeder primary schools will know that their efforts have been worthwhile.

10. When you have worked with Logo you start to question your approach to mathematics in the classroom. Is the mathematics the children are doing away from the computer building upon what they are doing in Logo? And vice versa – it is a two way process.

The need to monitor and evaluate a project is vital – they enable the initiative to have more momentum and allow the project to develop.

11. You have to be available and supportive at all times even though you are drinking your cup of coffee in the staffroom and someone needs help, which often happens when staff are involved in a new initiative. They want it to be successful and are often afraid of doing the wrong thing. If you want it to be successful you have to be prepared for all unforeseen eventualities. It is part of your commitment.

Denise had the support of the IT coordinator within her school as well as the PLUM coordinator from the LEA. The school IT coordinator had a wealth of expertise with regard to hardware, which gave Denise support between visits from the project coordinator and instant help if a piece of hardware malfunctioned. By the end of the project she had become 'expert' at managing the hardware.

12. Try to be sensitive to your colleagues' needs. You can often use too technical language. What you may consider straightforward may be highly technical to them.

Before their projects began, Denise and colleagues, John and Wendy had no specialist knowledge about computers. During the project this changed as they became more proficient with using the equipment and they attributed their success to the plain English which was used by the experts. They learnt technical names as their projects developed but none of them used technical language in discussions with colleagues. What they had learnt to use effectively was the language of Logo, which uses English within defined concepts.

The use of highly technical language acts as a barrier between the novice and the expert – it does not impress, rather it prevents others from wanting to take part in a new initiative.

Conclusion

This chapter has considered in some detail the use of Logo in mathematics teaching, specifically through programmable toys and screen-based Logo. The benefits for children are:

- increased understanding and use of mathematical vocabulary;
- in the linking of the strands of the mathematics curriculum, so that children can use knowledge and understanding acquired in one area, for example number, or shape, or space, use and apply it within measures, and extend their knowledge and understanding of algebra through further investigation. This can lead to accelerated learning in the particular areas of the mathematics curriculum included;
- the development of problem-solving strategies;
- the development of personal qualities through the need for children to collaborate, to persevere and to talk about their work.

CHAPTER 4

Using Concept Keyboards and Calculators

Concept keyboards and calculators may appear unlikely bedfellows in one chapter. Cockcroft (1982) devoted a whole chapter to calculators and computers. However, the introduction and use of concept keyboards and calculators into schools can be seen as exciting innovations. Some schools use both well, others will still be at the beginning stages, or, particularly in the case of concept keyboards, have rejected their use altogether. This chapter was written to show what can be achieved by one teacher in a school, with careful planning and with the support of other staff. The chapter falls into two sections: the first is about concept keyboards, mathematics and reception class children, the second is about the use of calculators with Years 3 and 4. The three teachers whose work is quoted wrote their accounts as part of award-bearing inservice training. The teachers' contributions are:

1. The use of a concept keyboard to enhance children's interaction with classroom environments.
2. Calculator work in the first school, with special reference to a Year 3/4 mixed class.
3. Introduction of calculators to a Year 4 class.

CASE STUDY

1. The use of a concept keyboard to enhance children's interaction with classroom environments, by Wendy Proctor

The information technology strand of the Technology orders (DES, 1990) gave all children the entitlement to use IT software and hardware. Whilst many schools now have a computer in every classroom, for others this has not been financially possible and a system of sharing hardware has been introduced. Wendy planned, implemented and evaluated the use of concept keyboards in the reception class, as part of an INSET course for Early Childhood Education. The innovation in her classroom was well received by her colleagues at school, her headteacher, parents and governors. The school continued its support of Wendy's work by purchasing more computers within the framework of an agreed school policy on IT.

The reception class had used the computer on a two-day per week rota due to limited availability of microcomputers in school. There was very limited software and a lack of development and cross-curricular work on Information Technology. The children had used programs such as 'PODD' and 'Lift Off with Numbers' which concentrated on spatial and maths activities. There had been a concept keyboard in school for about a year and the children had used commercially available programs where a press on the concept keyboard translated vocabulary onto a computer monitor. Although this satisfied the National Curriculum in Technology 1990, AT5/1, of children working with a computer, this was rather an uninspiring activity which led only to a dull grey print-out picture and there was little motivation to make this cross-curricular in a class topic.

I planned to achieve three aims:

1. To extend my own skill and knowledge of the most appropriate computers and the software for Early Years.
2. To implement the microcomputer as a resource for developing cross-curricular topics, involving the use of some structured play.
3. To ascertain its value in developing learning skills.

I was interested in exploring the potential values of the use of the computer with these children. I felt that I was underestimating the value of the computer and there were many more learning skills that could be developed. I believed that it would be possible to develop social, language, motor, reasoning and concentration skills as well as the understanding of mathematical concepts.

I chose to use the concept keyboard in conjunction with the BBC B computer and the programmable toy, PIP. PIP is a floor-crawling computer independent of any other microcomputer, designed to develop control technology, spatial awareness and mapping skills. (Wendy's use of PIP with her class is recorded in Chapter 3.) The topic, Houses, was chosen as it was an area to which young children could relate and develop from their own experience. The use of the Concept Keyboard and PIP ran concurrently through the topic. I was very concerned to establish the value of play within the Early Years curriculum at my school. By incorporating this into the Houses topic I felt that I could give it a purpose and a value. Like Froebel (see Bruce, 1987), I believe that play is not trivial but essential. I was confident that by structuring the activities on the computer and PIP the children could explore creative and imaginative play in a purposeful and problem-solving environment.

Wendy used both the concept keyboard and PIP within her integrated curriculum. Wendy shared Froebel's belief that play can be both child-initiated and child-directed. Also like Froebel, Wendy believed in the importance of a broad and balanced curriculum which includes mathematics. Planned activities for learning mathematical concepts through play was an important element in the EME project (Matthews and Matthews, 1990). This curriculum development project was funded by the Schools Council from 1974 to 1979, and the project's publication, *Early Mathematical Experiences*, was reissued as a third edition in 1990. It was a timely reminder, with the pressures of the introduction of the National Curriculum for Mathematics, of the mathematical needs of children aged 3 to 6. It describes the play experiences of young children and the mathematical concepts and language which can be used in a variety of contexts. EME identifies six basic concepts that are relevant at this stage of education. They are: matching, sorting, comparisons, ordering, recognition of shapes, invariances (or conservations).

Wendy described her planning for the children's activities with the concept keyboard. She used the software program Stylus, which has a concept keyboard facility which allows teachers to prepare their own overlays. This is a relatively simple procedure and one which can be learnt quickly. The program also has a talk facility, which allows children to hear text being 'spoken' by the computer. The voice simulator has an American pronunciation and, as it will 'mispronounce' words to English ears, children tend to find it a very amusing and most enjoyable facility. For children whose reading skills are not yet well developed, it can be very helpful as text can be 'read' by the computer without teacher intervention.

> The topic of Houses was introduced by discussion of children's own houses, activity rhymes and stories. Then I introduced the overlays which I had made for the concept keyboard. The children enjoyed using the overlay then asking the computer to 'speak' what they had written, using this facility on Stylus. This helped the children to read what they had written.

Wendy produced overlays which fitted onto the concept keyboard. These had pictures on them, drawn by her, which identified a particular classroom area, such as the building bricks or the sand tray, where Wendy wanted the children to work. The children were asked to press on the picture and this produced text on the computer screen. The text set a task. When the children were satisfied that they had completed the task they returned to the computer and pressed another picture, which gave more text related to the same task, perhaps a suggestion for recording what had been done. Some of the overlays gave suggestions for exploring an idea; others had a series of pictures which the children needed to press in the correct sequence so that the text was correctly ordered and the task could be completed following the instructions. Some overlays encouraged the children to write using the computer keyboard; here the concept keyboard overlay provided useful vocabulary which the children were free to use if they wished. The children worked in small groups on practical tasks, which involved them in making plans for carrying out their task. Written recording was on occasions completed collaboratively, on others each child produced their own writing. Thus, the computer was a classroom tool, which provided suggestions, or instructions, or asked questions. It also provided support for writing.

The first overlay encouraged children to write creatively and led to the construction of toy houses. The toy houses were initially made using large wooden or plastic bricks which encouraged the children to make decisions about shape and size of bricks to be used.

Properties of 3D shapes need to be explored through practical activities. Which shapes will stack? Which will only fit on the top of a tower? Which have flat, which have curved surfaces? Children need to discuss their findings, using mathematical language in context. Through exploration of the properties of 3D shapes, where the faces of the solids are considered, comes understanding of the nature and properties of 2D shape.

The second overlay was used to set a task:

> Can you build a wall with the bricks?
> Draw it in your house book.

This encouraged the children to use their knowledge and understanding of the properties of the shapes of the bricks in order to build a wall. Through this they explored the patterns which could be made with bricks.

Within the classroom there was a display of real building materials, such as pipes, slates and guttering. Stories about building houses, such as 'The Three Little Pigs' were used to promote an interest in building walls.

The third overlay produced instructions and questions. The children were encouraged to use this one step at a time, so that on completion of, say, the roof for the house, they returned to the computer to find out what to do next:

> Make a model of your house.
> Find a box like your house.
> Make a roof with some card.
> How many windows in your house?
> Cut out the windows from paper.
> Stick them on your house.
> Make a door.
> Find the shape for your drain-pipe.
> Make your garage from a box.
> Make your car from plasticine.
> Can you put a light in you house?

This led to a choice of creative materials, planning, science and mathematical and technology skills.

This overlay also encouraged the children to make a plan and to carry it out. The instructions stated what was to be made; no instructions about how to make it, what the finished result was to look like, were given. The children needed to use their knowledge about the properties of 3D and 2D shape in order to tackle the tasks.

There was a prolonged imaginative play activity at the finished 'road' model when the children added toy people and cars.

Wendy's role is important. She gave the children the time that they needed to enjoy what they had planned and produced. She showed how she valued what they had achieved, as well as giving the children the opportunity to evaluate their models through their play.

The next overlay involved the children in reading, writing, number recognition and counting. Rachel's printout was:

> My house has 4 windows
> My front door is green
> My front door is 34
> My home has a living room.

Rachel produced a drawing of her house with four windows and a green front door with the number 34 on it.

The fifth overlay involved the development of decision-making skills. The shape box contained papers cut into squares, circles, rectangles and hexagons.

> Go to the shape box.
> Choose big and little shapes.
> Can you make your garden?
> Now make your picture with pretty papers.

This overlay followed activities on 2D shape. The children produced pictures of houses, gardens and people, which used coloured sticky paper shapes which they had cut themselves.

Before the work from the fifth overlay was begun the children had experienced a range of activities involving the properties of 2D shape. They were able to sort and name the shapes, knew how many sides each shape had, and which had straight sides and which had curved. For many children their experience in the classroom of 2D shape is limited to the regular shapes, so that the irregular is unfamiliar. (Regular shapes have all sides the same length and each vertex, or internal angle, the same size.) Figure 4.1 shows common shapes, but not in their regular form. If children are encouraged to sort and classify shape through properties such as the number of sides, then they will build the concept 'pentagon', 'hexagon' and be able to classify shapes within their environment, whether regular or irregular.

The more able children used the computer keyboard to input the numeral in this, the sixth, activity. This followed work on comparison of heights. Jan's printout said:

> There are 6 people in my family.
> My Dad is tall.
> My Mum is the tallest.
> My brother is the middle size.
> My brother is tall.

Those who were not yet ready to use the numeral keys on the computer keyboard used the concept keyboard overlay to record the number of members in their family. They then painted or drew the appropriate number of family members. Sarah produced the following computer printout to accompany her drawing:

> My family has 4 people.
> This is my Dad.
> This is my Mum.
> This is my brother.
> This is me.
> Sarah.

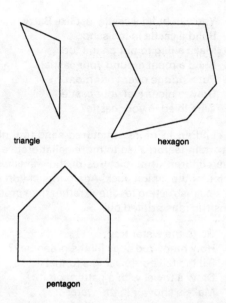

triangle   hexagon

pentagon

Figure 4.1 Children should be familiar with both regular and irregular 2D shapes

The children were able to use vocabulary from the overlay in order to produce the sentences shown. Wendy found that the layout of the numeral keys on the BBC B computer was difficult for some children to use (there is no separate keypad). However, the overlay included numerals so that children had a choice of using either the overlay or the keyboard to type in numerals as well as text.

The children in Wendy's class had had opportunities to use both the sand and the water trays in imaginative play, then Wendy had added structure, by making particular equipment available and by setting tasks. During the life of the Houses theme, the children were encouraged to use the sand and water as part of their imaginative and structured play, with open-ended tasks being suggested on occasions. Indeed, the sand tasks were triggered by a child designing and building a castle in the sand.

Whilst the following two tasks may appear very formal, they are an attempt to incorporate sand and water activities into Wendy's topic, through the use of the concept keyboard. Many of the smaller tasks involved mathematical vocabulary, such as the language associated with position, size, and quantity. Wendy wanted to encourage more cooperation between the children when they were working in the sand and the water.

> You can build a castle just like Barry.
> Build a castle in the sand.
> Make a flag to put on the top.
> Build a moat around your castle.
> Put a bridge over your moat.
> Draw a picture of your castle.
> Who lived in your castle?

This led the children to more structured sand-tray play. The building of castles with certain features led to more collaborative, constructive use of the sand. The children drew pictures of their finished castles and made accurate copies of the Union Jack. Again, the children returned time and again for the next instruction to follow, rather than producing a piece of text with all the instructions printed out.

> Go to the water tray.
> How many red cups fill the green box?
> Fill the tall bottle using a funnel.
> Draw a towel with a pattern on it.
> Make a shower in the water-tray.
> Find something that will sink.
> Make bubbles with soap.
> Find something that will float.

This followed discussion of the use and flow of water in the house and was based upon the children's suggestions. A collection of bathroom items was displayed and the print-out (to which the children referred during their play) reminded the children of their suggestions for water-play activities.

In another task the children were asked to use the play-house to arrange a tea party. The children made 'dough cakes'. There was much discussion, mathematical concepts of counting and matching and organization of who was invited and where they were to sit.

> Go to the play-house.
> Ask some friends to come to tea.
> Please give your friends some cakes.
> Please lay the table.
> Please wash up.
> Draw a picture of you having tea.

The outcomes of this part of the project were well received both within her own school and in dissemination through INSET to other teachers. Dissemination included Wendy showing a group of teachers, who wished to return to teaching after a career break, how to make overlays for concept keyboards and demonstrating how these could be used to enrich the children's learning experiences. For the children, five distinct outcomes have been identified.

a. The classroom working environment needed to be adapted so that the children had access to the materials that they needed for the activities. Materials needed to be stored so that the children were able to find what they needed. For some activities Wendy had to decide which materials to put out in order to give the activity the structure she intended. For example, when attempting the water-tray tasks, the children would need red cups, green boxes, bottles, funnels, soap and so on.

Activity areas within the classroom had clearly defined roles: there needed to be sand and water; the imaginative play area was set up as a house for this topic; the construction area of the classroom needed to contain the materials which the children would need for designing and making buildings; and children needed access to papers, crayons and shapes. From the children's viewpoint this gave clarity of purpose to the materials which were provided for use. It also encouraged the development of autonomy, as the children had responsibility for finding what they required and for clearing away again.

b. The children became actively involved in exploration and decision-making. Properties of items were explored and discussed. Children were encouraged to sort and classify, by colour, shape, size and so on, and to find a means of recording the results.

In busy classrooms it is not always possible for the teacher to discuss learning outcomes with the children. Data-handling charts can be used to provide a stimulus for class or group discussion. A simple record, which allows a group of children to place objects into agreed categories can be used by other children. The headings of such a chart could be as shown in Figure 4.2

Another group can then check the first, or set themselves new sorting criteria, such as comparing their sorting with that recorded by another group of children. Combinations of sorting criteria lead to using more sophisticated means of recording, such as a four-region Carroll diagram, shown in Figure 4.3.

The added sophistication in using concept keyboard overlays and a program such as Stylus is that the children can choose the talk facility so that an electronic voice 'speaks' what they have written on the computer screen. Thus the development of the associated mathematical language proceeds in tandem with the

These things float	These things do not float

Figure 4.2 Simple data-collection record sheet

	Floats	Does not float
Red		
Not red		

Figure 4.3 Four-region Carroll diagram

practical activity. Wendy reported that the children in her class loved the electronic voice, especially when it 'mispronounced' something, according to them.

The overlay which involved using knowledge and understanding of 2D shape, offered other opportunities for making decisions. Which shapes did the children decide to choose? How could these be incorporated into their pictures? In this way the children made active choices, dependent upon their preferences: their knowledge about the properties of the shapes and which ones they wanted in their pictures.

c. The children developed their skills of collaboration. They planned, made and evaluated together when working in the sand to make castles. In the play-house the children were able to choose who to play with, to make decisions about where children were to sit, with what to lay the table, checking that there was enough crockery, cutlery and dough cakes for everyone. For the teacher this represents an opportunity to observe whether the children are using one-to-one correspondence to check quantities, whether they count how many children there are and compare that with the amount of cakes. Are the children able to use their understanding of number in order to calculate how many more cakes would be needed if two more children joined or if three left?

Collaboration was encouraged, for example through the children being involved in model-making. The outcome of this activity was that the children combined their models to make a street scene. They decided to add toy cars and play people to this and enjoyed using the street scene in imaginative play.

With an adult to join in the play, opportunities can arise for the children to develop their understanding of direction, with the cars travelling along the street, then making left or right turns. Again, mathematical language development can take place. Children need to hear and use positional words such as on, under, behind, in front of, to describe their own movements or that of objects during play. The Mathematical Association's book, *Maths Talk* (1987a), refers to the importance of mathematical language being used during activities in order to help children to develop their mathematical thinking strategies.

d. The children experienced both those activities which differentiated by outcome and those which differentiated by task. Differentiation by outcome is possible where the task set is an open one, that is, there will be a range of possible solutions. Children are asked to find a solution to a problem and are encouraged to use strategies and skills for problem-solving. Activities which differentiate by outcome can be used in mixed ability teaching. Examples of the former can be found in the first, second and fifth activities, where children made decisions about the materials to use: shapes, sizes, quantities, design. They were able to demonstrate what they knew and understood about the properties of the shapes that they had chosen. Differentiation by task occurs where there is a known outcome. The task is usually a closed one and this is suitable for children of similar ability and can be used to assess a particular skill or the acquisition of particular knowledge.

Activities such as these can be enriched through discussion between children and between teacher and children. Such activities lend themselves to discussion during recall sessions, when children are encouraged to tell other children what they originally planned to do, why and what the outcomes were. Other children can question and add suggestions for further investigation. Again, the opportunities for developing mathematical language are present, particularly where an adult takes part in the conversation.

In one activity, some of the children were ready to find the numerals they needed from the computer keyboard and to use comparative language from the overlay to describe the heights of their family members. Others needed to use the concept keyboard overlay to supply the numeral and to identify their family members. The task was differentiated, that is, Wendy chose whether children used the concept keyboard overlay or the numeral keys on the keyboard according to their ability. The outcomes were individual and unique to each child.

e. Some of the tasks involved counting and numeral recognition. We use numbers to identify nominal, cardinal and ordinal values. for example, a bus number is a label, or nominal value; it distinguishes one bus from another. Rachel's house number is 34, which is ordinal number, whilst her house has four windows, the four representing a cardinal value, or the number value of the set of windows (as discussed in Haylock and Cockburn, 1989.)

Children need to distinguish between these uses of number, to understand that the context in which the numeral is used denotes how it is being used, whether as label, as an order or as an amount. Jane understood 6 to represent an amount – how many people in her family. We do not know if she was the youngest or the sixth member (ordinal).

The use of the concept keyboard in this topic led to mathematical experiences for the children in number, shape and space, measurement and data-handling. A common theme throughout all the activities was the opportunity to develop mathematical language through practical activities and to use the concept keyboard as an aid to reading and writing using such language. This matches well with the basic concepts identified by EME as matching, sorting, comparisons, ordering, recognition of shapes, and invariances. Wendy provided a rich diet of experiences across the mathematics curriculum.

Wendy had used concept keyboard overlays as a teaching support. The children used overlays which offered different experiences:

- as a starting point for exploration;
- as instruction: where to work; what materials to use; what to do;
- as a means of recording work completed.

These uses freed her, as teacher, to work with other groups of children, so that one group could use the concept keyboard whilst Wendy worked with other children. One overlay for the children in Wendy's class could produce the equivalent of a day's work. Each group, pair, or on occasions, individual child would use the overlay. This dedicated the hardware to the use of the concept keyboard so that the computer would not be available for any other purpose. However, the children became familiar with the use of the computer through using the concept keyboard. The computer acted as an introduction to the conventional computer keyboard through the use of the numeral keypads by those who were able to recognize numerals in this format.

As an innovation, Wendy's project was considered to be very successful both by colleagues within her school and by other teachers in her LEA. The report of what the children and she had achieved contributed to the school debate on IT. This use of IT encouraged children to use classroom environments for structured play activities through which they acquired and extended mathematical understanding. The main drawback to this work was that some of the text in the overlays appeared in the account of the case study to produce stilted play situations, which dictated to the children what they were to do. In practice, perhaps because the classroom was a stimulating learning environment, the children interpreted their tasks in an imaginative manner, and used the computer as another helpful tool, rather than as a teacher substitute.

A look back to the Cockcroft Report (1982) paragraph 411, which refers to secondary education, shows how far and how fast schools have changed their practice during the past 10 years. This paragraph refers to the need for computer software to contribute to mainstream mathematics work and not just to be 'extras'. Using a concept keyboard and a program such as Stylus gives both teachers and children the opportunity to use 'content-free' software, where the design of the work to be undertaken is left to the teacher and the child. This is a very different scenario from that found by Cockcroft in 1982, where, (paragraphs 407 and 408), the programs in use were generally of the drill-and-practice variety for number, or for recognition of numerals and letters and were much less likely to be interactive or to encourage problem-solving. Today there is a wealth of good quality software available, which can be of the content-free variety, or encourage problem-solving or investigations, such as Monty from Slimwam 2. This software is relatively inexpensive and can encourage a rich and varied programme of work for mathematics.

Calculators

The debate about the use of calculators in schools began in the mid-1970s as their price began to fall. The debate ranged over whether children needed to learn their number bonds and tables, whether or not to teach algorithms for long multiplication and division, whether children would become less or more numerate with the advent of the calculator, and what the needs of industry were. Paragraph 375 of the Cockcroft Report (1982) contains reference to the range of views being expressed by the late 1970s, early 1980s. Paragraph 377 of the same report states:

> From all the studies the weight of evidence is strong that the use of calculators has not produced any adverse effect on basic computational ability.

And paragraph 378:

> We wish to stress that the availability of a calculator in no way reduces the need for mathematical understanding on the part of the person who is using it.

Shuard (1986) refers to evidence that the majority of primary children have access to a calculator or own one and see older people using them. Children will today see electronic tills in use in shops and will be used to receiving a print-out from the till, which gives total spent, amount tendered and change to be given. This is in marked contrast to parents' and teachers' early shopping experiences when shop assistants either totalled the bill 'in their heads' or wrote out the bill and used a combination of paper and pencil and mental methods to find the total. Today's children are, in the main, used to electronic ways of calculation and see this in common use in the wider world outside school. This in no way means that children do not need to know and be able to use their number bonds and table facts.

What, then, of the use of the calculator in the classroom? Brissenden (1988) suggests that it can take three roles: that of teaching aid, learning resource and tool. Evidence from The PrIME Project (Shuard *et al.*, 1991) has shown that children aged 6 to 7 who were not taught standard algorithms for the four rules, but who had free access to practical materials and calculators, developed understanding about several mathematical concepts which they would not normally have met until they were older. These included understanding about very large numbers, understanding something of negative numbers and operating with them, and some understanding of decimals and fractions. In addition they developed a clear conceptual framework of place value. Walsh (1991) quotes case studies of children's achievements from the PrIME Project and raises the issue of how teachers can be supported to respond to the challenges of the findings of the PrIME Project.

The following two case studies come from two teachers who carried out their action research as part of their participation in an INSET course. Reference is made in both studies to the use of the constant function. The following instructions for setting the constant function are known to work on some calculators; however, some of today's calculators will not accept these instructions in order to produce number sequences:

For addition: press clear
key in 1 + + = 0
key in 1 = = = etc
The calculator will produce the sequence 1 2 3 4 etc.
Similarly 2 + + = 0, then 1 = = = will produce the sequence of odd numbers, 1 3 5 7 etc.

CASE STUDY

2. Calculator work in the first school, with special reference to a Year 3/4 mixed class, by Andy Smart

I work in a four-class 5 to 9 first school. As staff we have found that the requirements of the National Curriculum in relation to calculator work have brought about the need to introduce the calculator at an earlier age than was previous practice. As a result we undertook a review of calculator work in the school. The diary of events within the review of calculator work was as follows:

Summer 1991
1. Review of calculator use within school. Decision made to introduce calculators earlier in the Year 1 and 2 class rather than in the Year 2 and 3 class.
2. New set of calculators purchased. Introductory calculators (ie, simple calculators) moved to Year 1 and 2 classroom.
3. Review of available teaching resources.

Autumn 1991
1. New aims developed and work started in planning to extend calculator skills at the top of the school considered in the light of pupils' experience as they progressed.

Spring 1992
1. Maths course taken and a calculator resource pack produced as part of the course.
2. Calculator experiences as covered in previous years completed.

Summer 1992
1. Implementation of additional extended work using calculators.
2. Proposed review of progress across year groups.

The review was discussed both at staff meetings and informally with the Year 1/2 and Year 2/3 teachers. It was decided to resource the work by buying a new set of calculators suitable for use in Years 2/3 and move the set of 'first calculators' previously used there into the Year 1/2 class. In each set there were twelve calculators.

Williams and Shuard (1987) refer to simple four-function calculators being useful tools for young children to use, as soon as they understand the meanings of the signs +, – and =. Children can use these to investigate number bonds, patterns and as a check to mental and paper and pencil calculations. However, as Hughes (1986) states, children need to know which mathematical function it is appropriate to use in a problem-solving activity and, as Skemp (1989) points out, children need to recognize whether or not the answer is sensible.

A review of calculator material resources in the school and aspects of calculator work, problems and difficulties regularly encountered was made by the three staff concerned. Aims were discussed in order that a coordinated policy was developed. The Year 1/2 teacher was helped and supported in her introduction of calculator work. A variety of materials from several published schemes were well used in school, some of which mentioned and supported calculator work. However, we all felt that additional material would be required if the calculator was to be fully realized as a potential tool in mathematics. We had purchased a series of calculator books some years ago and these were successfully in use by the older children. We felt that these formed a useful resource which complemented, supplemented and expanded existing maths work. A further resource was the booklet produced as part of the Maths Certificate course which we called, 'Can Calculators Cover Ken's Curriculum?' and which grouped together sheets from published books and other sources, aimed at NC Level 3. This provided a wider selection of photocopiable resources and adaptable sheets and ideas.

It was agreed that calculator work was an important part of the mathematics curriculum, though reservations were expressed regarding its introduction before children in Year 1/2 class had grasped the basic knowledge of mathematical concepts and skills. We felt, however, that the teacher's judgement was imperative here, to ensure calculators were introduced at an appropriate stage in children's progress. Record-keeping was also recognized as very important so that pupils would be able to progress and avoid repetition of tasks already completed and understood after they transferred to another class. This was a particular issue with classes of mixed age groups.

Once a child has grasped the meaning of addition and subtraction and has some understanding of symbolic notation, then calculators can be introduced. However, there are available very simple fun calculators, which have large key pads and are intended for use by very young children. One or more of these could be available for use in the imaginative play area of the reception or nursery class, before the children have reached the stage of using numerals in calculations in a formal, symbolic sense. Perhaps the area is a hairdressers or a garage. Children can use the calculator in role play when making out pretend shopping bills. A calculator with a till roll which produces a print-out could also be used, or the constant function could be set so that it could be used as a counting device, perhaps to record each time someone comes into the play area. Young children, like their Years 1 and 2 counterparts, will have seen children and adults using calculators outside school. Having a calculator available in reception and the nursery allows children to role play using a calculator, to develop the appropriate language.

Within my own class I did not, of course, benefit form the pupils starting earlier in their work with calculators. However, I have tried this term to extend their work according to ability and age and to use the calculator as a 'tool' to extend their mathematical achievements. I kept a diary during the Summer Term 1992 and show below the order of the activities which were used and their effectiveness.

1. Calculator practice for Year 3 pupils and less able in Year 4, from a photocopy master, which included number and shape activities. The pupils had already been introduced to calculator work and were provided with revision work where necessary. Techniques for constant addition, repeated division or multiplication by a constant number were taught and practised. This proved a useful exercise as it carried over into maths investigative work on number patterns and tables by some groups of children. Children coped noticeably better with larger numbers when assisted by the calculator. Some of the younger or less able children enjoyed playing number games. Children worked in small groups with an ancillary helper who on occasions acted as referee.

2. Groups working individually on sheets to practise division.

3. Calculator technique for constant pattern of division; this included work on the recognition of decimals and what these mean.

4. Calculator games, a) to find highest, lowest possible totals of three numbers chosen from a list, then to find all the possible totals of any three numbers; b) games with various levels of difficulty. I used ancillary support with small groups of children.

5. Practice at estimating results; this involved subtracting 10 or 100 from a given number, then checking result with the calculator.

6. Shopping, which introduced work on rounding numbers to the nearest whole number.

7. Calculators used to calculate averages for science experimental work – reinforcement of the meaning of long strings of numerals following the decimal point was required, also of the rounding up and down of results.

   The games and work sheets reinforced knowledge and skills for estimation, place value, the four rules by varying the rules and sets of numbers in some of the sheets. Shopping activities were used with most pupils to introduce the meaning and reading of decimal numbers and rounding them to the nearest whole number. This linked well with work in science involving timing and measuring three runs by toy cars and models down ramps. Pupils used the calculators to find an average figure. This inevitably gave a long string of numerals, following the decimal point, which they realized meant very little and could therefore sensibly be rounded to a whole number or to two decimal places in the case of distances in metres. This was considered a 'fair' answer as it could be measured out in metres and centimetres.

8. Using decimal numbers in multiplication to two or three decimal places, by finding the sides of a perimeter of area 24 square centimetres. Children were encouraged to adopt trial and improvement

methods; this was for average and above average pupils. Initial teaching required. Small groups worked with the ancillary helper to assist with frequent questions.

The use of decimal numbers in multiplication involved teaching new knowledge and skills, but it was, I felt, the next step in progression from decimal answers in division. The work stimulated much discussion among the pupils, particularly looking at the 'size' of the numbers and who was the closest. Pupils were grouped for this in similar ability groups.

9. Children set their own problems for each other then attempted to solve them.

This followed on from (8) above, for those pupils who had grasped the concept. This resulted in the use of estimation before trying out numbers, especially if the number of attempts was limited.

10. Good guesses, involving estimating the size of the answer when a two digit number is multiplied or divided by a one digit number. The calculator is then used as a check.

At the time of writing, the whole school review on using calculators has not been completed. It is the case, however, that the children have enjoyed the work tackled and have progressed further with both calculator work itself and, especially in the case of the more able pupils, with their mathematical knowledge. This is particularly so in their understanding and use of decimals, an area not previously tackled to any depth with most Year 4 pupils, except for the most able. It has been useful to be able to tackle decimals as the need has arisen, for example, in relation to science experiments.

In future, I will have a longer period of time in which to do this work, unlike this year where the changes have been crammed into one and a half terms. Next year I intend to use more problem-solving practical work both with and without the use of calculators. I want to concentrate upon the pupils making decisions about the process to be used in a particular problem-solving situation. I also want to make more use of the calculator in science, geography, history, investigations, in fact more cross-curricular use, as it has been evident to me this year how beneficial the use of the calculator is across the curriculum.

It is interesting to follow the gradual development that Andy and his colleagues went through. At first, the calculator was seen as a tool for the children to use to help them to practise the four rules. However, it was seen from experience that there was spin-off in number and pattern investigation work and that the children were able to use the calculator as a learning resource as well as a tool. With the introduction of rounding to the nearest whole number (see 6 and 7 above) the calculator was being used as a teaching aid. Thus, within this account can be seen the three uses of the calculator to which Brissenden (1988) refers.

re is reference in the report to the children managing large
bers much more successfully with the aid of the calculator.
is reflects the findings of the PrIME Project and those of Denise
nd her colleagues in Chapter 3 on using Logo with children in Key
Stage 1. There is also reference to children estimating the size of
an answer in multiplying or dividing a two digit by a one digit
number, then using the calculator to check. Williams and Shuard
(1987) refer to the need for children to learn their tables in order to multiply single digit numbers mentally. With the aid of calculators children can identify patterns, such as multiples of five or
ten, etc., which go far beyond those normally investigated. That
is the power of the calculator. It allows children to extend their
experience into what used to be uncharted territory for primary
children, to perceive patterns in number which would not normally be available to them through the usual methods of generating number pattern.

Here, then, is the report of Steve Bryant, who introduced the use
of the calculator into the curriculum for his Year 4 class.

CASE STUDY

3. Introduction of calculators to a Year 4 class, by Steve Bryant

During a recent conversation with a friend, we discussed mathematics
teaching. The discussion typically turned to the use of calculators in the
classroom. My friend was very sceptical about using calculators and felt it
affected standards of teaching and learning. He also believed that children
should reach a certain age before calculators were made available to them.
My beliefs were different. I believed that calculators should assist children
with their mathematics and that their use should not be limited to a
particular age range any more than the use of IT should.

With the help of a short questionnaire I established that, amongst my
colleagues, although everyone appeared to recognize that calculators could
make an important contribution to mathematics teaching, their use was still
varied. Calculators were seen as a resource, useful for checking results
when using large numbers, but children needed to understand the computation process. My colleagues either used calculators occasionally in
their teaching or not at all; they wanted help with devising suitable classroom activities which incorporated calculators. Most of the children in
Years 3 to 6 were familiar with calculators as they had access to one at
home.

My experience of using calculators in the classroom was very similar to
that outlined above. I had heard of their potential but had never estab-

lished what contribution calculators could make nor what they could be used for. My Year 4 class appeared typical and showed that there was a wide range of different understanding and experience of using calculators: some children felt confident in using a calculator for simple addition and subtraction of hundreds, tens and units, others had never used a calculator.

I decided that children did need to experience the use of calculators to assist with their mathematics. They needed to be taught how to use them so that they could be used to help the children to improve their mathematical ability, not to reduce their computational ability or just to find the answer. In planning, my objectives were:

1. To use calculators in the work on division already planned.
2. To use calculators in work on the four rules, using what the children already knew and understood as the starting point.

I wanted the children to understand that the use of calculators does not reduce the need for mathematical understanding. In fact, I believed that it would be necessary for the children to understand the number operations in order that they could use the calculators. The calculators were to be used as a check for answers already derived. The work with calculators would also reinforce the children's understanding of place value and number bonds, particularly with division.

3. To use calculators for investigating number and number pattern.
4. To use calculators as an aid when estimating.

I hoped that this would encourage confidence in work using large numbers and open-ended work.

5. To use the constant and repeat function appropriately.
6. To use calculators to explore negative numbers, decimals and very large numbers.

The essential point would be that using open-ended ideas would enable children to extend their work as far as they were able.

7. To use calculators in mathematical games.

I wanted them to experiment, to investigate their ideas, to become more confident with calculations, with handling questions and problems. This would involve children using and applying their work in number and algebra.

The children were enthusiastic about using calculators and were prepared to listen attentively. Each new operation was explained carefully and children soon understood that each entry on the calculator was a single operation, including the operation and equals signs.

In Hughes (1986) there is a reference to children understanding the equals sign as a command to the calculator to calculate. This is a different meaning from that of the equals sign in algebraic equations where it refers to the balance between the two sides of the equation. Children need to understand both meanings.

I encouraged the children to provide their own calculators but realized later that some of these were unsuitable. The calculator needed to be a basic one with the main mathematical functions, but some provided by the children were too sophisticated and proved difficult to operate. The school calculators were solar powered and some of the power cells were broken during the term, rendering the calculators useless.

Some of the calculators which children will see used at home will be the much more sophisticated scientific or graphical calculators which are now available relatively cheaply. These would be useful at Key Stages 3 and 4, but would be too complex for most usage at Key Stages 1 and 2.

The children became efficient at checking their calculations very quickly. For example, in using the multiplication square (see Figure 4.4), effective use of the constant and repeat functions was applied as a means of checking mental calculation. I observed how quickly the children had taken to using the calculator as assistance in their mathematical work.

Whilst the constant function will produce number patterns, careful study of the multiplication square in Figure 4.4 shows that the pattern of multiples of three is correct as far as the normally learnt tables, that is to 3x10. After that, errors have crept in. Similarly, in the pattern of 4 this is correct as far as 4x15, and then the next three terms are incorrect. Other errors can also be found. The use of the calculator set with the constant function to produce, say, the pattern of fours, would allow a child to spot errors and to correct this work.

The most dramatic change came with the children's use of large numbers. The children were asked to:

- keep notes about any ideas about patterns which emerged;
- record any reasons or predictions about any results or answers;
- choose one or two number patterns and focus on what happened when the pattern was extended.

This was the first time that most of the children used thousands and tens of thousands. Their handling and confidence with these large numbers was most encouraging for me, their teacher.

A similar result was found by Andy, see above, and by Denise, reported in Chapter 3. The use of the calculator encourages children to investigate much larger numbers than would normally be used. Children can produce these numbers through forming sequences of numbers in a pattern, or through calculations using the four rules. The calculator improves confidence with handling such numbers as children learn how these behave.

Multiplication Square

20	40	60	80	160	131	141	50	181	200	220									410
19	38	57	76	95	114	134	150	172	190	209									380
18	36	54	72	90	108	127	144	163	180	198									360
17	34	59	68	85	102	120	136	153	170	182									340
16	32	41	64	80	96	112	128	144	160	176									320
15	30	45	60	75	90	105	120	135	150	185									300
14	28	42	56	70	84	98	112	126	140	154	166								280
13	26	39	52	65	78	91	104	117	130	143	156								260
12	24	36	48	60	72	84	96	108	120	132	144								240
11	22	33	44	55	66	77	88	99	110	121	132								220
10	20	30	40	50	60	70	80	90	100	110	120								200
9	18	27	36	45	54	63	72	81	90	99	108								180
8	16	24	32	40	48	56	64	72	80	88	96								160
7	14	21	28	35	42	49	56	63	70	77	84								140
6	12	18	24	30	36	42	48	54	60	66	72								120
5	10	15	20	25	30	35	40	45	50	55	60								100
4	8	12	16	20	24	28	32	36	40	44	48	52	56	60	65	70	74		80
3	6	9	12	15	18	21	24	27	30	32	36	39	42	44	47	50	53	56	60
2	4	6	8	10	12	14	16	18	20	22	24	26	28	30	32	34	36	38	40
1	2	3	4	5	6	7	8	9	10	11	12	13	14	15	16	17	18	19	20

Figure 4.4 Multiplication square, partially completed

The investigations with number patterns illustrated the children's ability to make calculations and make predictions.

Figure 4.5 shows how Josh has started by generating a simple pattern of adding the counting numbers from 1 to 10. Then he has formed a prediction based upon previous experience, then tested this using the calculator as an aid to calculation. He continues by forming an hypothesis that this pattern will be repeated in other decades and shown this to be true for the 80s.

In the example shown in Figure 4.6, Kate has investigated pattern in multiplication. She has generated a pattern which for the

94

$1 + 2 + 3 + 4 + 5 + 6 + 7 + 8 + 9 + 10 = 55$

$11 + 12 + 13 + 14 + 15 + 16 + 17 + 18 + 19 + 20 = 155$

I think that the next numbers are like

$55 - 155 - 255 - 355$ and on.

$21 + 22 + 23 + 24 + 25 + 26 + 27 + 28 + 29 + 30 = 255$

$31 + 32 + 33 + 34 + 35 + 36 + 37 + 38 + 39 + 40 = 355$

$71 + 72 + 73 + 74 + 75 + 76 + 77 + 78 + 79 + 80 = 755$

There might be the same numbers in a pattern like from $755 - 855 - 955 - \ldots$ and on. Like this on the calculator can add it and add up bigger numbers

$81 + 82 + 83 + 84 + 85 + 86 + 87 + 88 + 89 + 90 = 855$

Figure 4.5 Josh's number pattern, which he used to predict further number sequences

$12 \times 8 = 516$

$12 \times 80 = 5160$

$12 \times 800 = 51600$

$12 \times 8000 = 516000$

$12 \times 8001 = 516012$

$12 \times 8010 = 516120$

The sums go up in a pattern because it the same number with something added on

Figure 4.6 Kate's multiplication number pattern, where she changed the sequence

first four terms increases by a multiple of ten each time. She can see a pattern, but does not identify what has happened, that 72 is multiplied by another power of 10 each time. Nor does she comment upon the last two results, where her pattern has changed, perhaps because the numbers involved are outside her normal experience. The pattern changes, and begins a new sequence which, if continued, would behave in the same way as the previous one. Does Kate realize that she has changed the sequence? Kate would benefit from more experience of exploring number patterns in order to develop her understanding of place value.

Some children experimented with the calculator to find out about some of its functions.

The first investigation shown in Figure 4.7, to find a multiplication which uses all the digits 1 to 9, just once, shows the result and a description of Matthew's pleasure. However, it would be help-

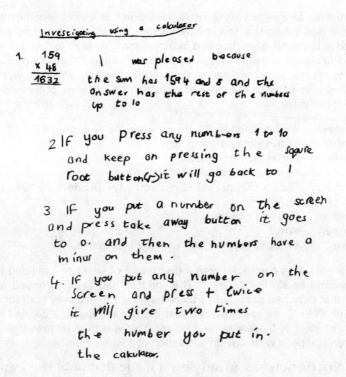

Figure 4.7 Some investigations, which involved the use of the calculator

ful if the children were encouraged to record their rough working to show the processes which have been used to get to that result. How was this answer obtained? Was it by random inputs until one worked? Was there a logical process?

The other answers refer to questions where the children were asked to explore some of the functions of the calculator. In 2, Matthew had made an interesting mathematical discovery, but it would appear that he did not understand the mathematics that lay behind it. In 3, he had produced negative numbers. Did he understand what these were or why this had happened? In 4, he had used the constant function in order to produce multiples of two. If he had continued with that, Matthew would find that he could produce the sequence of odd or even numbers, dependent upon the starting number. For example, 1 = = = = = = would produce 1 3 5 7 9 11 13. 2 = = = = = would produce 2 4 6 8 10 12, and so on. Each of these questions contained interesting mathematics which Matthew would benefit from exploring further.

> The most positive aspect of the implementation of this work was the discussion that was generated. The children wanted to talk about numbers, they wanted to show me what they had found and they wanted to find out more. One particular conversation was about the division of 33 by 3. Two children came to tell me, with confidence, that their calculators were not working. They had entered what they thought was correct, but were presented with a line of numbers.
>
> | | |
> |---|---|
> | *Teacher:* | It's 3 divided by 33, is that what you're putting in? |
> | *Karen:* | 11 this time it turned up. |
> | *Teacher:* | Is that the right answer? |
> | *Karen:* | Yes. But the calculators are wrong! |
> | *Teacher:* | Wait a minute. What did you say? Divide 3 by 33? Is that right? |
> | *Laura:* | You can't divide it. |
> | *Teacher:* | Why? |
> | *Laura:* | Because you've got 3 which is less than 33. |
>
> The conversation continued with a discussion of whether 3 divided by 33 is the same as 33 divided by 3. The children had been surprised at the result that they had obtained as there had been a recurring number (3/33 = 0.09090909). They soon realized that the two inputs, ie, 3 divided by 33 and 33 divided by 3, were quite different. This was the first time that most children had dealt with a decimal fraction of a whole number.

The observation has already been made that until children understand the meaning of the operation signs they cannot use a calculator successfully. This discussion was useful. For Steve it highlighted the children's misconceptions about division. For the children it clarified what division as an operation meant.

The language which the children used was thoughtful and relevant. One child, when working at magic squares, referred to a 'vital' number. The word was discussed with the class and children gave their own reasons why a number was 'vital':

10	You put things in tens.
	10x10 = 100. The numbers have more noughts.
	The metric system.
5	5 is like 10 because it is a good number, like 2x5 = 10.
	It is easy to add.
0 to 9	0 to 9. All other numbers are made up of those digits.
100	Crossing numbers out to make other numbers.
0	There in 100, 10, 20s.
12	Because it was the number they used to group in like £sd and inches.
11	Because it changes 22, 33. It's a double number.

The work on estimation also stimulated a great deal of discussion and resulted in the idea of 'What is a million?'.

Proposals for future planning needed to be drawn up. The important aspect for future planning was the integration of these ideas into the general mathematics curriculum of the school. There needed to be a school policy on the use of calculators which would also need to address:

- progression, continuity and balance across year groups;
- identification of the use of the calculator within the school's mathematics scheme;
- integration of calculators into other subject areas, eg, technology and science;
- how calculators would be resourced;
- care and maintenance of calculators;
- advice to parents who wish to provide calculators for their children on which ones would be suitable.

The use of calculators in the classroom does open up great opportunities and potential for future work. A close analysis of work might identify where the greatest benefit exists for children's learning. Rather than simply checking work and routine computation, the calculator might be used as an aid to thinking in identifying relationships between numbers or in handling complex calculations.

Calculators have been shown in the above two examples to be useful as teaching aids, learning aids and as tools. Their use helped to identify children's misconceptions and allowed Steve the opportunity to help the children to correct these. Their main function was to:

- aid calculation;
- introduce children to very large numbers;
- introduce children to negative numbers;
- act as a check for prediction, calculation or estimation;
- aid with rounding up or down to the nearest ten, hundred or to a simpler decimal;
- allow children to explore number patterns.

The observation of both teachers that children were able to manage much larger numbers than would normally be within their expectations has been replicated in other studies.

What emerged for both schools was the need for a clear policy statement on the use of calculators which all staff would agree to implement. This would facilitate a developmental approach to the use of calculators in the mathematics curriculum and also identify cross-curricular uses of the calculator.

Conclusion

This chapter has considered the introduction of concept keyboards as an aid to learning in the reception class and the use of calculators within Years 3 and 4. The need for clear policy statements for the use of IT and calculators throughout the school was identified. The use of the concept keyboard showed that children could be encouraged in structured play activities which involved mathematical concepts and skills. Both the calculator projects showed children's greater ease with using large numbers and negative numbers, their improved understanding of place value and their enhanced skills in prediction, estimation and rounding.

CHAPTER 5

Using Themes and Topics

In this chapter, the use of themes or topics in mathematics teaching will be examined. The starting point for many LEA courses on planning for the National Curriculum has included the use of themes or topics as a vehicle through which it is possible to plan to include other curriculum areas. This was suggested by ASE (1989) who demonstrate a model for planning and teaching for the core curriculum which could utilize topic work or which could be subject-specific, depending upon the teacher's professional judgement.

How have teachers planned and taught mathematics? This chapter contains four case studies; two describe a theme or topic approach and two describe specific subject teaching. The effectiveness of these two planning models is examined in this chapter and other planning models are considered. All four teachers wrote these accounts as part of an INSET course assignment. The four accounts are as follows:

1. Identification of specific mathematics teaching points to be developed through a cross-curricular topic of pattern.
2. Themes of 'Children's Games' and 'Birds'.
3. Pattern in number and shape and space.
4. Mathematical Investigations.

CASE STUDY

1. Identification of specific mathematics teaching points to be developed through a cross-curricular topic of pattern, by Val Pendleton

I wanted my Year 5 children to improve their understanding of number patterns. In the school where I worked, other members of the Year 5 team felt unsure about using an investigative approach to mathematics teaching. I believed that the only way to move forward was to promote a package of materials which used investigations and games in the study of number patterns.

My class consisted of 32 children. In September over half of my class had poor understanding of number; some found place value difficult and could not distinguish between hundreds, tens and units; many could not identify patterns in numbers; very few children had previous experience of investigative methods; most found difficulty with identifying patterns and recording results; many of the children could not read or interpret a calculator display and could not interpret the decimal point. I believed that my 'package' or scheme of work needed to address these issues and should draw upon existing school resources, such as tapes, slides, interlocking cubes, coloured rods, calculators, pin boards, games, etc. I also decided to draw up a draft requisition order and to demonstrate that there was a need to build up the school's resource bank.

My objectives for the children's learning were:
1. To work across Levels 2, 3 and 4 of the National Curriculum. To be flexible enough to allow for extension work, as necessary.
2. For the activities to be enjoyable. To utilize investigative techniques wherever possible. For maths to be fun.
3. To enhance the children's understanding of number and number patterns, through observation and prediction.
4. To use practical equipment, such as interlocking cubes, coloured rods, counters, pin boards, calculators.
5. To increase the children's range of strategies for mental arithmetic, through using knowledge of pattern, eg, tables, observation of arithmetic and geometric pattern growth.
6. To encourage children to devise their own patterns.
7. To enhance understanding of algebraic functions.
8. To encourage group- or partner-based activities.
9. To apply mathematics to solve problems.

For the children, then, there was a need to change attitudes towards mathematics, to encourage them to enjoy their work. Inability to identify the meaning of numbers, to interpret them, to know what each digit represents, would lead to failure with computation as children would have no concept of the 'size' that an answer should be. The use of practical materials, such as interlocking cubes, pin boards and so on, would help the children to understand how the number system works. Hughes (1986) argues that children's understanding of arithmetic is dependent upon their ability to transfer from concrete experiences to written, symbolic representations of calculations. This understanding grows with the development of observation and prediction, in searching and identifying number patterns. This will assist with recognizing known or predicted number patterns and enable children to use either or both mental and pencil and paper methods for calculation. Brissenden (1988) points to the need for the teacher to use a questioning technique which encourages the generation of problem-solving activity rather than prompting a 'correct' answer. This can identify a range of responses to the task set, rather than just one which the teacher deems 'correct.'

> In evaluating the project I found that the children working at Level 2 found it difficult to commence investigative work, to find patterns and record results. This was due, I believe, to their lack of experience. As their knowledge grew they became more confident. They were helped initially by others in their group but became more adept at finding patterns with experience. Placing the less able child to work with the more able worked well. It was motivating for me to observe the less able find sequences in patterns and to see their confidence and enthusiasm grow.

Carol was assessed as working at Level 2/3. She tried an investigation which involved continuing the sequence, identifying the pattern and finding the twentieth and the hundredth terms. The following is a transcription of her work.

The pattern:

```
1 *           2 *           3 *           4 *
              ***             *             *
               *           *****             *
                              *           *******
                              *             *
                                            *
                                            *
```

Carol found the following

Term	1	2	3	4	5	6	7	8	9	10
Counters used	1	5	9	13	17	21	25	29	33	37

She found that the difference between a pair of counter patterns was 4 and the first 10 terms. She found these through using counters to make each pattern. Carol was unable to go beyond the tenth term. She needs more experience of continuing sequences, identifying pattern and of making and testing predictions so that she will begin to form generalizations which will help her to find any term in a sequence.

Sarah (Level 2) investigated rectangular numbers. She found the following pattern and put in the difference between consecutive multiples:

$2 \times 4 = 8$
      7
$3 \times 5 = 15$
      9
$4 \times 6 = 24$
      11
$5 \times 7 = 35$
      13
$6 \times 8 = 48$
      15
$7 \times 9 = 63$
      17
$8 \times 10 = 80$
      19
$9 \times 11 = 99$
      21
$10 \times 12 = 120$
      23

From this Sarah predicted that the next term in the series would be 23 larger than 10 x 12. She commented:

> I have noticed in the first column it goes up in ones and the second column it is the same and the third column it goes even odd even odd and the fourth column goes up in the two times table.

Careful questioning of Sarah would help her to note that the product of two even numbers is even, of two odd numbers is odd and that the pattern in the fourth column is of odd numbers increasing by two each time, not the two times table. She has already observed that the products alternate between even and odd. Discussion with Sarah would help her to express her observations more precisely and to use mathematical language correctly. She has identified patterns in her results and formed a prediction which could be tested. An extension for her could be to investigate products where one multiple is even and one odd, to predict whether the result will be odd or even and to check by multiplying.

> All pupils thoroughly enjoyed the investigative approach towards learning. They looked forward to lessons and asked to complete work at home. Their understanding of basic number and their ability to find patterns increased considerably.

The children's ability to express their mathematical ideas improved. They were able to find their own words to express quite complex ideas, without as yet always using more sophisticated, mathematically correct language. John, working at Level 3, compared the measurement of one edge of a cube with the number of centimetre cubes needed to build it. The following is a transcription of what he recorded:

Edge of solid cube (cm)	1	2	3	4	5	6	7	8
Number of cm cubes	1	8	27	64	125	216	350	512

He wrote:

To find the measurement you times the number 3 times. So in your brain or on a calculator you press

eg $1 \times 1 \times 1 = 1$
eg $(2 \times 2 \times 2) = (4 \times 2) = 8$

He had discovered that the relationship between the term number and the resulting number of cubes was the term cubed. He had also realized that the result could be obtained by using mental calculation or through the use of the calculator.

As Haylock and Cockburn (1989) state, children need to build up cognitive connections when they are learning mathematics. Cognitive connections are made through combinations of practical experience with concrete materials, use of appropriate language including specifically mathematical terms, using pictorial representations and the use of symbols to represent calculations. The use of practical equipment is essential for children to have both the manipulatory and visual experiences from which they can identify patterns and form generalizations.

Two children worked together on this investigation, using a calculator to help them.

e numbers 1 2 3 4 5, they had to find the largest and
possible answers for ABC X DE. The following shows their

432	543	321	412	145
x51	x21	x45	x35	x23
22032	11403	14445	14420	3335

They wrote:

> We have made the numbers as big as possible and number 1 is the biggest answer.

The children had found the largest product from those that they tried. However, they had not found the largest possible product. Then they had to find the smallest possible product:

154	134	543	243	123
x32	x52	x21	x51	x45
4928	6968	11403	12393	5535

They wrote:

> We have made the numbers as small as possible and number 1 is the smallest answer.

Again, the children have identified the smallest product from those that they tried rather than searching for the smallest possible. They did not notice, from the previous results, that they had already found 145 x 23 = 3335, which was a smaller product than any other found. The language used, whether spoken or, in this case, written on a worksheet, must be accessible to the children. It must be understandable. These two children identified the largest and smallest of their results. It is suggested that they had not fully understood the nature of the task. To find the largest and smallest possible would involve more searching (and pattern spotting) and this can be daunting to children who are still unsure about their mathematical ability.

During the project, Val encouraged the children to write some plays about number. Val asked the children to imagine that an alien had landed on earth who did not know what numbers were. Emma wrote a play where she described numbers and how they are used. She identified those who need to understand how numbers work for their jobs.

Describe what a number is to an alien, by Emma
I was in my back garden playing when suddenly a shadow came over me. I

looked up to see what it was. When I looked up a purple blob jumped and landed beside me.

We...bonk
Who are you?
Me Blob who are you?
I am called Emma I have two sisters as well.
What are two?
Two is a number that we use.
What do you use them for?

People use them for all sorts of things like prices, car number plates, door numbers and clocks. We use numbers to help us to count. Some people use numbers in their daily jobs or life.

1   postman
2   milkman
3   police
4   cricketers
5   golfers
6   jockeys
7   runners
8   books
9   diaries
10   music and many more things.

I am using numbers to list things.
Oh look at the stars. I must go perhaps I will come and see you another day.
Bye.
Bye.

Emma sees numbers as labels, for car number plates – this is the nominal aspect of number. She also identifies numbering as a useful way of identifying objects in a list, this being the ordinal aspect. Cardinal values are implicit in the list, for example, cricket scores and the milk bill. Compare this with Anna's play. Anna described the counting numbers and how these are ordered, or cardinal and ordinal aspects. She identifies where numbers are used for a purpose.

Describe a number to an alien visitor, by Anna

Martian: Bleep, Bleep, Bleep.
Me: Ah! W-who are you?
Martian: Bleep, I am SJ, I am from Mars.
Me: How many people are on board your space ship?
Martian: Bleep
Me: Don't you know what numbers are?
Martian: No, what are numbers?

Me:	You use numbers to help you count, on doors, in racing, on clocks, dates, prices and so on.
Martian:	What like?
Me:	Well, you get numbers on calculators.
Martian:	What do calculators do?
Me:	They also help you to count.
Martian:	What is the first number?
Me:	1
Martian:	Oh, what comes next?
Me:	2,3,4,5,6,7,8,9,10
Martian:	Like this? 1,2,3,4,6,5,7,8,9,10
Me:	Not quite, try again.
Martian:	1,2,3,4,5,6,7,8,9,10
Me:	Well done, you can count numbers.
Martian:	Now I know how many people are on board.
Me:	How many?
Martian:	10.

Writing a play about number is an exciting way to encourage children to describe what numbers are. At the beginning of her account, Val described over half her children as having poor understanding of number. Both Emma and Anna display some understanding of how the number system works and its place in everyday life.

> Art lessons helped to consolidate the concept of visual pattern and the children produced Aztec designs and mosaics. This work was stimulated by the use of slides depicting pattern in nature. Cross-curricular links worked well, particularly in music, English and art. Support from the specialist teachers was essential. However, meetings to discuss the work proved difficult to organize.

Val has documented the beginnings of a process of change as she moves towards a more investigational approach to mathematics teaching. This approach, which utilizes other areas of the curriculum, can be found in some of the newly published mathematics schemes such as Nelson Mathematics (1991). In this scheme art, music and PE are considered to be useful vehicles through which children can experience and identify patterns and pattern-making. Val's account has shown that her children can be involved in a cross-curricular approach to mathematics, which has also allowed the mathematical development to be clearly identified within the children's experience. She was able to produce activities which were stimulating, encouraged investigation and which also allowed breadth and balance across some elements of the curriculum, particularly mathematics, art, music and English.

CASE STUDY

2. Themes of 'Children's Games' and 'Birds' by Jill Harmer

I recently began a mathematics INSET course. The other course members and I experienced real anxiety at the beginning of the course: perhaps our maths ability was not sufficient to find the right answers all the time. However, this feeling dissipated when we realized that in one sense it was to be a journey of exploration and discovery, to find out how maths can be fun, enjoyable and rewarding. We were being taught to think for ourselves, rather than being told what to do.

I wanted to follow this approach with the children in my class: to seek patterns, to recognize, extend and generalize patterns as well as for children to generate their own. Patterns form the underlying basis of mathematics; they are the source of structure of the subject, through number, algebra, geometry and logic, and the National Curriculum reflects this in its structure.

At present, the school I work in has four classes: class 1 for R and Y1, class 2 for Y2 and Y3, class 3 for Y3, Y4 and Y5 and class 4 for Y5 and Y6. There is a staff of seven including a non-teaching head and two part-time teachers. I have responsibility for class 3, a group of 27 children, aged 7 to 10. For the summer term, 1992, we chose, as a whole school topic, 'Children's Games'. For the second part of the term I also used the topic 'Birds'.

The children in my class were used to working independently, due to the maths scheme we were using. They worked at their own independent levels and at times did practical activities either in pairs or a group, but this allowed for little investigational work. The children assessed their success by the number of red ticks on the page. I wanted to change this attitude. I introduced problem-solving sessions where I encouraged the children to think, estimate, experiment, assess and evaluate. I found that their confidence and enthusiasm for being able to solve problems was gradually increasing and it was this aspect that I wanted to explore further. I believe that children need a constant source of opportunities to tackle mathematical problems in an investigative manner using mathematical thinking and language – to be able to cooperate and find a variety of solutions, then evaluate which is the best. Children need the confidence to experiment and not to be disillusioned if it does not work, but to use that as a stepping stone to further exploration. Children need to develop their mathematical language in order to be able to describe to others what they are doing and why.

To begin, I produced a topic web, shown in Figure 5.1, and then I made an appropriate selection from the programmes of study for mathematics, which took particular account of AT1 and included:

- using trial and improvement methods;
- simplifying difficult tasks;
- looking for pattern;
- making and testing hypotheses;
- proving or disproving hypotheses.

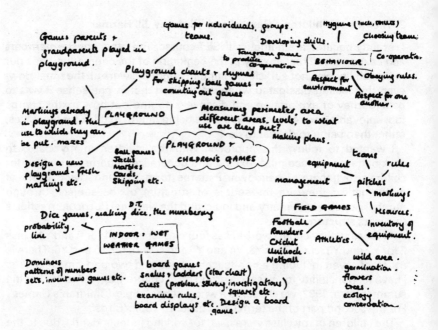

Figure 5.1 Teacher-produced topic web, showing possible mathematical activities and personal and social development skills

The National Curriculum programmes of study endorse identification of pattern in number and algebra as major areas. Children who were used to working from a published scheme where success was measured by the number of red ticks for correctly worked 'sums' would not be used to searching for and identifying pattern. Nor were these children used to using the problem-solving strategies listed above under 'AT1 Using and Applying'. These appear two high-risk strategies for Jill to adopt. Desforges and Cockburn (1987) state that investigations are high-risk enterprises so that it is possible that classroom processes will convert open problems into predictable routines or that they will become safe, dependable, low-risk activities, so that both teachers and children feel safe and confident in using this approach. Since the publication of the Desforges and Cockburn research, National Curriculum orders have required that teachers of Key Stage 1 introduce their children to problem solving strategies through the programmes of study for AT1. Can this way of working be introduced to children in Y3, who are not used to it?

This topic needed time for the children to discuss, to show what they already knew and understood and to identify the aspects which individuals and groups would like to pursue. One of the purposes of the topic was to make playtimes happier through exploring different avenues of play and highlighting the importance of cooperation with, and consideration of, others.

I felt that children's games would be a good vehicle for investigative maths because it should generate enthusiasm, excitement, total involvement and enjoyment. It was important to encourage the children to discuss moves, the correctness of answers and different strategies, so I hoped to stimulate discussion between groups of children and also between children and teacher. Playing as part of a team, children need to learn to cooperate in order to play effectively – even children playing against each other are cooperating in playing the game. Playing games demands involvement, especially if children want to win.

Two sessions each week were allocated to these investigational activities. I kept a diary of implementation.

Week 1
1.   Oral discussion; what do children think of playtimes. Good and bad points. Encourage children to express themselves clearly and to listen to others.
      What can they remember about the layout of the playground? Make a class plan.
2.   Large selection of children's games available in the classroom.
      Discuss which games children have at home. Which are their favourites?
      Consider snakes and ladders in detail. The board: how many squares? How many snakes? How many ladders? What are the rules for play?
      Children work in groups and play one of the board games.

Week 2
3.   Play a cooperation game which involves making a square from a range of pieces. In order for all the children in the group to be able to make their square, children need to offer pieces to each other.
      Discussion of how and why groups succeeded.

Children need to be able to cooperate for successful group problem-solving. Most board games encourage competition; however, it can be argued that in order to compete it is necessary to cooperate with each other. In this game, each child depended on others to help to supply the pieces which they needed in order to complete the square. Without cooperation, and collaboration, the game would have failed.

4.   Make a large snakes and ladders board, from one to one hundred. Discuss the layout of the hundred square. Children note that for snakes

and ladders the numbering starts at the bottom left and zigzags from left to right, with 11 above 10, thus;

```
21 22 etc.
20 19 18 17 16 15 14 13 12 11
 1  2  3  4  5  6  7  8  9 10
```

Discussion of patterns of numbers on the board and where and how they occur.
Odd and even numbers.
Children to seach for other number patterns on the board.

The numbering on such game boards does not follow the convention of a hundred square, which has decades placed on columns or rows, thus;

```
 1  2  3  4  5  6  7  8  9 10
11 12 13 14 15 16 17 18 19 20
21 22 etc.
```

or

```
1 11 21 31 41 51 61 71 81 91
2 12 22 32 42 52 62 72 82 92
```

These represent just two of the many possible hundred square frames which can be formed. For children to become adept at searching for pattern it is helpful if they use a variety of formats for number squares so that the physical arrangement of the numerals is recognizable in any format.

Week 3
5. Discussion of rules for games. Board games, PE games, playground games.
    Why do we need rules?
    Children look at the games in the classroom: are their rules useful?
    Children play games in groups, this time including chess, snakes and ladders, ludo, Mastermind, crossword, What' Rummikub, and others which the children have brought in.

Do the board games have common rules? For example, some games insist that a six or a double (if two dice are used) must be thrown in order to start play for each person. Are there rules which penalize a player, perhaps through a missed turn? Do all players need to follow the same route around the board? Children can compare the rules of different games, consider why these have been designed in this way, and then consider if they are fair to everyone.

6. Look at large foam dice. Language of probability. Discuss the properties of a cube; sides, faces, edges, corners. Count the spots.

Predict which number will be face up after the dice has been thrown.

Throw dice 20 times, as a class activity, and make a tally of the results.

Week 4

7. Children try some dice investigations, considering possible combinations when using more than one dice.

Week 5

8. Make a net to form a cube.
How many tabs needed?
Decide on best design.
Each child makes their own dice.

This is an interesting activity for children to do, particularly if they are then asked to evaluate the effectiveness of their dice when used in games. It is highly probable that such a dice would be noticeably biased. Children can explore what is meant by 'fair'.

Week 6

9. Review snakes and ladders board.
Make up own designs for a game.

The children used their experience of playing games in order to make their own.

Simon produced four ideas for playground games which could be marked out on the ground. The first was a long-jump game, to be played along a two metre line. The children could measure the length of their jump to a degree of accuracy commensurate with their ability. The second was a hopping snake game where a long wiggly snake with a number line on its back needed to be marked out on the ground. Children hopped along it. This could be used in many ways, for example, children could work their way along the snake, by addition of two dice, or subtraction, or by multiplication. The snake could be used starting at 1 or at its highest number and the children working back along it. The third idea was for a larger than usual version of hopscotch. The fourth was for a chess board to be marked out. Simon suggested that the children themselves could be used as the pieces.

Sarah invented a jungle adventure game which used a grid on which the game board was set out, and a dice (see Figure 5.2). She set the starting number to be thrown on the dice as do most commercially produced games. Many children must consider throwing a six to have some magical property as it allows them to start moving around a game. Sarah chose five. Perhaps the work which she had already done on throwing dice and tallying the results had helped her to see that, if the decision is taken for there to be a starting number, then what that number is will not matter if a fair dice is used.

Figure 5.2 Sarah's jungle game

Sarah does not make it clear whether or not the 'five' needed to start the game also identifies the size of the first move. She has understood that board games involve pleasant and unpleasant moves.

Peter invented a game based on map grids. He labelled the columns with letters and rows with numbers, giving each square a label, such as F9 or E3. On the grid he drew a map with some treasure which could only be collected by following the grid instructions for the trail. He gave the map references for the trail, clearly and concisely. If followed correctly not only did the players collect the treasure, but they could imagine that there was some dynamite to blow up the 'treasure' square.

Week 7
10. Times tables on a one hundred square. What number patterns can children identify? Which can be predicted?

Week 8
11. Problem-solving on a hundred square. Looking for number patterns to solve problems.
12. Bird Maths. Using coordinates to make pictures on graph paper.

The work involved plotting given pairs of coordinates in the first quadrant. Lisa produced the piece of work shown in Figure 5.3.

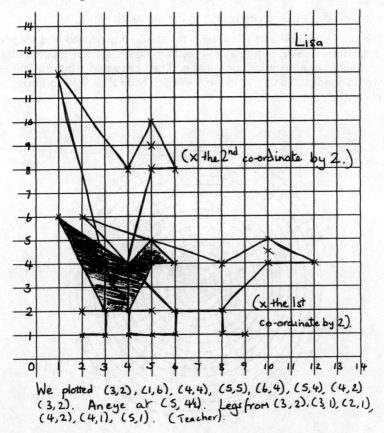

Figure 5.3 Lisa used pairs of coordinates to produce the birds

She then experimented with multiplying one coordinate then the other. As can be seen, this work was completed accurately.

Paul produced the work shown in Figure 5.4 using a circular grid. Here the same birds were plotted. He found difficulty with correctly plotting the bird with enlarged second coordinate so that the bird's back is wrongly positioned. However, in subsequent work, Paul produced the same bird in each quadrant, which involved him in taking account of negative numbers (see Figure 5.5).

Louise used parallelogram paper to plot the same bird; the results are shown in Figure 5.6. She found placing her axes on the paper more difficult than in the other cases. She wrote of this work:

> 'I have enjoyed the parallelogram one. It was hard but fun. I also injoyed Doing the fat one. I suppose it was like a challenge. I also Done the thin one. I would love to Do it again when I'm about 13.'

Of the Bird Maths investigations Jill wrote the following.

> During the second part of the term the children produced bird shapes on graph paper, using coordinates. They then looked at what happened if they multiplied one or other coordinates. They predicted what they thought would happen, then they plotted these points on to parallelogram paper to check their predictions.

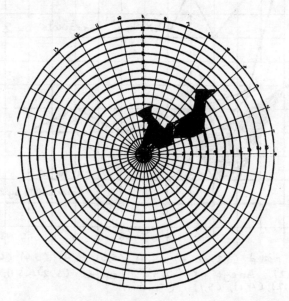

Figure 5.4 Paul used pairs of coordinates on a circular grid

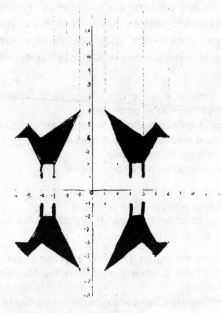

Figure 5.5 Paul used all four quadrants

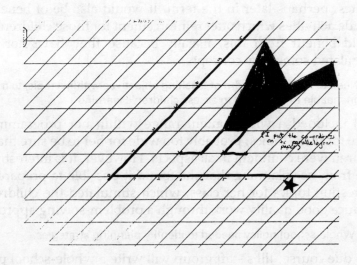

[I put the co-ordinates on the parallelogram paper]

Figure 5.6 Louise used parallelogram paper to plot the coordinates to produce this bird

Prediction before plotting the points would encourage the children to look for pattern and shape of outline. It is important that children check that they have plotted the points correctly and that the shape either fits their prediction or that they have identified why it differs from what was expected.

Week 9
13. Review language of probability: sure, likely, probable, certain, definitely, impossible, no chance.
Refine children's use of appropriate mathematical language.
Open-ended discussion about probability.
Formulate a probability scale.
Make an illustrative probability scale.

14. Experimental work with coins and dice.
Draw up probability questionnaires.
Encourage children to make an hypothesis for the probability of a particular event occurring.

The children certainly enjoyed the investigative approach. My evaluation of the effectiveness of this programme of work led me to the following conclusions for my teaching;
i. This approach needs a bank of extension activities for the children and me to draw upon.

The children who tried the Bird Maths activities so successfully would have enjoyed some extension activities based on coordinates, perhaps later in the term. It would also be of benefit to include activities which offer reinforcement for those children who would benefit from this, usually because they have not fully assimilated some new concepts.

ii. Need to limit the breadth of teaching objectives within a topic, to make it manageable to teach and to assess children's learning.

Jill included a wide content range within her programme of study for these topics, probably too wide for her to be sure that the children were confident in all aspects. However, it is interesting to note from her planning that she found it possible to prepare two interesting topics for her class, which stimulated the children to produce good quality work through a problem-solving approach.

iii. Whole-school policy needed to identify planning strategies.

In due course, Jill's staff group will write a whole-school policy which includes the development of problem-solving strategies through the school, supporting teachers in what would be for many a very different way of teaching. Burton (1984) identifies four stages of problem-solving; entry, attack, review and extension. Staff would need to consider the implication of this model of problem-solving and how it differs from their normal, scheme-based approach to teaching mathematics. Staff development needs would require consideration and a careful programe of support, agreed and funded.

iv. As children gain in confidence, more open-ended questions and tasks can be introduced.

Some of the tasks set were open-ended, for example, designing a cube to be used as a dice. Other tasks relied upon children using their knowledge and understanding of similar systems in order to devise a new one; for example, the board games which Sarah and Paul made relied heavily upon the rules for games likes snakes and ladders.

v. More careful planning to provide for differentiation required.

All the children attempted all the activities. Some of these were open-ended which gave the teacher the opportunity to see evidence of the children's present stage of development. The cube design offered this, with those children who showed perseverance more likely to find a more unusual net of a cube, whilst others would use the conventional net which they had met in their published scheme mathematics.

Open-ended activities offer children the opportunity to think divergently and creatively and to find their own solution. The teacher can differentiate by outcome. Other activities may have a more limited range of outcomes; the teacher can then differentiate by task, choosing the activity which is most suitable for a particular child's learning and development.

vi. Children need to be encouraged to develop different methods of recording.

It is important that children record their mathematical thinking for a purpose. This could be so that they have an *aide-mémoire* of steps that have been taken during an investigation or it could be that the recording will form part of a classroom display so that the children can compare different forms of recording. Recording in rough, perhaps jottings in a notebook or on a piece of paper whilst doing a computation, should be encouraged. To present just the 'polished' version, without the thinking and working which have been undertaken, will mean that both teacher and child lose the opportunity to check through the process which has been used.

Domoney *et al*. (1993) consider that children should be encouraged to show their recording to each other, to talk about their work and to share what they have done with their teacher so that recording is seen to be purposeful.

The two approaches to teaching mathematics through topics that have been presented here were different. The first took a theme which could be used across the curriculum and in subject-based work. For mathematics this meant that children used the theme of pattern to investigate numerical and algebraic patterns. Other subject areas supported this work through the exploration of pattern in art, music, nature and so on. The children used their knowledge and understanding of writing plays in order to explain what numbers are. Thus the theme or topic, whilst taught in individual subject sessions, enabled the children to make inter-disciplinary links whilst the 'subjectness' of each subject area was retained. The good quality mathematics outcomes which the children achieved are evidence that this approach worked for this teacher and this class of children.

The second approach was different. The first topic of Children's Games had been chosen as a whole-school topic in order to try to improve the relationships between the children during play-times. It was seen as a means to improve cooperation and collaboration. Jill used it to develop the children's understanding of the need for rules, of fairness, of collaboration. Her topic was much broader than she reported here, as she concentrated upon the mathematical aspects of her teaching in this account. The children used knowledge and skills from other subject areas when completing some tasks. For example, the board game devised by Sarah used story-telling. As the player moves around the boards so an adventure story is told. Peter, in his map game, used geographical knowledge and skills. He devised a map reference system and there was a story within the map and the instructions which he produced. The mathematics outcomes were of good quality and the children showed understanding of pattern. The initial planning which Jill undertook for these topics was very thorough – it is suggested that this is the essence of success. She had devised her programme of study for the children to follow and then broken this down into weekly sessions. She had mapped it into the five attainment targets for mathematics which would assist with assessment. With such careful planning for both the children as learners and for herself as teacher she ensured that the content was stimulating, relevant, developmental and rigorous and that it matched the required Programmes of Study for the National Curriculum.

CASE STUDY

3. Pattern in number and shape and space, by Caroline Worthington

My class comprised 29 Year 2 children, of whom 20 were boys. In order to introduce a more investigational approach to my teaching, I chose to use the topic pattern. I wanted to introduce the processes involved in searching for pattern both in the arrangement and location of shapes and in number sequences. I chose to try this approach during the summer term of 1992, particularly because I would have two first-year students attached to my class for a three-week school experience. This would provide an opportunity for extra support for my children and also give the students the opportunity to experience such an approach to teaching and learning.

The learning objectives for the children were to encourage them to:

1.   look for pattern in shape
2.   look for pattern in number sequences;
3.   develop spatial awareness;
4.   learn through informal yet challenging mathematical investigations;
5.   work together, sharing ideas, discoveries and, where appropriate, equipment;
6.   work independently, following a predetermined strategy of approach;
7.   realize the implications of different kinds of movement (rotation, flip, etc.).

With the above objectives in mind, I sought suitable materials. Some came from my memory, some from INSET materials and some from published materials. I found *Brainwaves* (Scholastic, 1989), *Bounce to it* (Hatch 1984), *Developing Mathematics in Your Classroom* (Maths Development Team, 1988) and *Mathematics in Action* (Maths Development Team, 1990) very helpful.

My original planning contained too many ideas for the time available, so I decided to restrict my planning to that of shape and space and its overlap with number, and the first activity in the number section as this activity was linked to the development of skills used in mental arithmetic (see Figure 5.7).

The first investigation used was 'frogs and toads'. This was a variation on the well-known 'frogs'. My main objectives for this were to encourage the children to search for pattern, to discuss their results with each other, to identify procedures and to tabulate results. I intended this to be a whole-class activity with the children sharing ideas.

Starting points

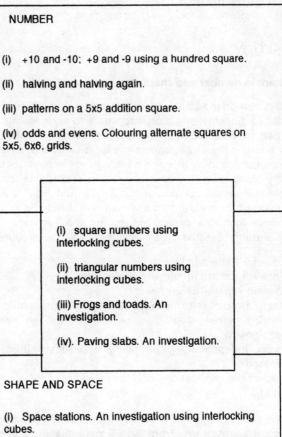

NUMBER

(i) +10 and -10; +9 and -9 using a hundred square.

(ii) halving and halving again.

(iii) patterns on a 5x5 addition square.

(iv) odds and evens. Colouring alternate squares on 5x5, 6x6, grids.

(i) square numbers using interlocking cubes.

(ii) triangular numbers using interlocking cubes.

(iii) Frogs and toads. An investigation.

(iv). Paving slabs. An investigation.

SHAPE AND SPACE

(i) Space stations. An investigation using interlocking cubes.

(ii) Pentominoes, polyominoes.

(iii) Bus stop. A mathematical game.

(iv) Tessellation of plane shapes.

(v) Transformations. Concept of area using a simple tangram.

(vi) Triangle patterns.

Figure 5.7 Teacher's original topic plan, showing the interrelation of activities across number and shape and space

We began with three chairs in a line with a 'toad' sitting on one end chair and a 'frog' on the other, thus;

       *   *   *

   frog   toad

The children were given the task of reversing the positions of frog and toad following two rules;

moving or sliding across into an adjacent empty chair;
hopping over an adjacent frog/toad into an empty chair.

This task was completed by the two volunteers in three moves. I recorded on the board:

| 1 frog | 1 toad | 3 moves |
| 2 frogs | 1 toad | ? moves |

We discussed whether the number of moves needed for FF*T to become T*FF would be the same as for 1 frog 1 toad, more or less. All agreed it would be more but there were differences of opinion as to how many more.

Mike thought, 'It would take five moves because there are three people'. Leanne said, 'It would take four moves because there is one more person so it would take one more move'. Many of the children seemed to like this piece of logic and so agreed with Leanne.

Different children directed the hops and slides until it was proved by exhausion that five was the minimum number of moves. I added this information to the board. David said, 'The number has increased by 2'. Mike said, 'The number [of moves] are both odd numbers'.

I was interested to see whether these observations would influence the children's predictions for the next task of reversing positions for three frogs and one toad. A few children guessed it would take six moves this time, but a substantial number thought it would be seven because, 'I counted it in my head', 'I worked it out in my head', ...'from the 3 to the 5 it has gone up 2 so the next one must go up 2'.

As before, the children directed the movements of the frogs and toad until they were satisfied that it was the least number of moves. When I added '4 frogs 1 toad' to the board, there was a unanimous prediction of nine moves because, 'Nine is two more than seven'. The children were thrilled when their prediction proved correct. The pattern on the board was now:

1 frog	1 toad	3 moves
2 frogs	1 toad	5 moves
3 frogs	1 toad	7 moves
4 frogs	1 toad	9 moves

I pointed out that in each case the number of moves was the number of frogs multiplied by 2 and then plus one or $[(y \times 2) + 1]$. Only the more able children could cope with this. They and I worked out that 9 frogs and 1 toad would take $[(9 \times 2) + 1]$ or 19 moves.

The children had identified number patterns and used this to predict the next outcome; they had all enjoyed the activity. I set them the task of trying again, this time with two frogs and two toads, FF*TT. They tried with chairs and children, then using cubes. It proved to be far more difficult but a few children managed this in the minimum of eight moves. I chose not to take this any further at this stage as the children were unlikely to be successful.

This activity demonstrated that the children were able to search for and identify number pattern and to form a prediction. As Skemp (1989) comments, children are delighted to find that their predictions are proven correct by subsequent events. The excitement of forming a prediction based upon previous experience, of testing it and proving it correct can encourage children to see the inherent, aesthetic beauty of mathematics.

A positive attitude towards mathematics comes from successful outcomes of tasks. Caroline had achieved this with her children through their first investigation as they discovered the power of number pattern to help to form predictions. However, at this stage, algebraic generalizations proved far too abstract for most of the children to comprehend.

The next activity, paving slabs, was concerned with paving around a pond, and seemed to follow on from frogs and toads. I explained that frog and toad wanted a new pond to swim in. Each side and corner was to be surrounded by paving slabs to make a neat border. Using squared paper the children coloured in one square unit for the pond and then in a different colour shaded in the slabs (see Figure 5.8). We recorded the number of slabs needed for one, then two, then three square units.

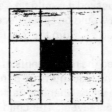

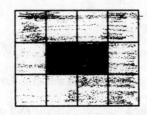

Figure 5.8 Paving slab investigation outcomes

1 square unit needs 8 slabs
2 square units need 10 slabs
3 square units need ? slabs

Many children saw the +2 pattern and predicted 12.

At this stage I introduced the possibility of other arrangements, using interlocking cubes to demonstrate which combinations were the same and which were different. Would the number of slabs needed be the same? What about ponds using 4 square units? If slabs cost £2 each, which arrangement for a 4 square unit pond would cost the least money?

The children worked individually. They recorded their results on squared paper, showing pond designs, slab surrounds and costings (see Figure 5.9). They found that the square design was the least expensive. As this work brought in the need to use concepts of area, I was interested to hear the children's reasons why the square arrangement was the cheapest of the four possibilities.

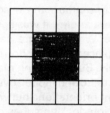

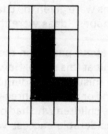

Figure 5.9 Paving slab investigation: different arrangements

Peter said, 'That one is bunched up into a square but the others need one more slab to go into the sides'. Melanie said, 'The L shape has to go into the corner.' Nick said, 'The others are spread out'. Tamara wrote, 'The square pond costs the least amount of money because it was not irregular and there were no squares sticking out'. Mike wrote, 'I think Frog and Toad bought the [square] swimming pool because it is less money. It is less money because it is in a square and the other swimming pools go in and out'.

I was pleased with their work. They had consolidated their understanding of the processes involved in spotting number patterns. They had also discovered that when variables are involved (shape of the pond) these affect the outcome.

The children had also learnt that different arrangements of squares can have the same area but different perimeters. Tamara showed understanding of the terms regular and irregular. The other children also understood that the square arrangement was the most compact, but, at this stage, did not use the mathematical vocabulary of 'regular' and 'irregular' to express their ideas.

Through this investigation, Building Shapes, I planned to develop conservation of shape and to increase the children's spatial awareness. Through making shapes with interlocking cubes, I tackled the concepts of rotation and reflection. I wanted the children to understand that the resulting shapes could be in any position in space or seen from any angle when suspended in space. I also wanted the children to work collaboratively by sharing ideas, talking about the shapes that they made and comparing shapes whilst working together in groups in a challenging situation.

I began by holding up one cube in the air so that the children could see the same shape from different angles. It was agreed that only one shape could be made from one cube. When I progressed to two cubes many children thought that two cubes placed together horizontally were different from two placed together vertically. But, following many examples of how the same pair of cubes could be rotated and flipped over to make shapes which looked different in their different orientations but were still the same shape, it was agreed that two joined interlocking cubes could only make one shape. In groups of four, the children were given the task of finding the maximum of possible different shapes, using three joined cubes, then four then five. For each number of cubes, groups were given the challenge of finding the maximum number of different shapes. Ideas were then pooled and the results tabulated on the board.

I did not ask the children about pattern in the results as it is a complex one and would be too difficult at this stage. However, the children enjoyed this activity. After the initial misunderstanding they became adept at discriminating between the same or different three-dimensional shapes. It was encouraging to see that those children who had poorly developed numerical concepts and skills had considerable success with this activity. As an approach to investigating types of movement, I found this activity ideal and would use it again.

It is recognized that children's performance in number aspects of mathematics may well be different from their performance with shape and space concepts. This is because number activities involve the left hemisphere of the brain and spatial thinking the right. Haylock and Cockburn (1989) point to the original profile components for the National Curriculum (DES, 1989a) which had number with algebra and measures, and shape and space with handling data, thus identifying the areas as being different. Within the new orders (DES, 1991b), this distinction has been removed as mathematics no longer has two profile components and has been reduced to five attainment targets from the original 14. However, many children do show a marked difference in performance between the two areas. Traditionally, boys have demonstrated greater ability in shape and space than girls. As there were so many more boys than girls within this class it may be that the traditional effect was more marked. However, all children need to become adept in both shape and space and number.

As a follow-on to the previous activity based on three-dimension shapes, I decided to develop the concepts involved by introducing a similar activity using plane shapes (interlocking 'squares') to investigate pentominoes. This was a class activity. We investigated the number of different shapes which could be made using one, two, then three squares. Results were tabulated on the blackboard. After a few guesses for the number of shapes possible from four squares, the task of finding out was set as a small-group activity. Groups then compared their results which were recorded pictorially on the board and the total tabulated. The task of finding the total number of shapes possible from five linked squares was set as an individual one with the understanding that children could share ideas if they wished. Each child had a sheet of squared paper on which to draw their pentominoes.

Most children preferred the challenge of working alone. I kept a running commentary on the highest 'score' so far, which spurred the children on. One child found 10. At this stage, the children felt that there could be no more so I told them that there were in fact 12 possible pentominoes. This provided a new incentive and soon all 12 had been found.

It was encouraging to see how most of the children had learned the concept of rotating or flipping over the shapes, a spin-off from the previous day's activity with three dimension models (see Figure 5.10). However, a few children had made a shape which they did not know how to draw on squared paper. They needed a gentle reminder that, with a slight rotation it could become a shape which was much easier to record.

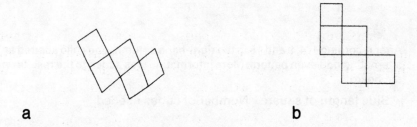

a   b

Figure 5.10 Rotation of shape a) shows that it is the same as shape b)

Whilst some activities can be organized for group participation, children also need to be able to work independently. Successful independent work depends upon motivation, confidence, perseverance and understanding of the demands of the task. However, when working independently, children will work at different rates. Desforges and Cockburn (1987) show that even when each child knows exactly how to proceed, the time taken to complete the task can vary by as much as 400 per cent. This has major implications for classroom organization and for the range of extension or reinforcement activities available.

My main objective for the Square Numbers activity was to use work on shape to try to spot patterns in numbers. First of all, we clarified what we meant by a square. One interlocking cube was placed flat on the table and we described the uppermost face as being square. One interlocking cube was one square whereas the next sized square (2 x 2) used four cubes (see Figure 5.11).

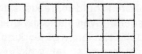

Figure 5.11 Growing squares, to show square numbers

I recorded the results in a table on the board and then invited the children to explore further by themselves, recording their information in their own table and pictorially on squared paper. Using interlocking cubes their task was to make increasingly larger squares (3 x 3, 4 x 4) and try to spot a pattern in their results. The results were:

Side length of square	Number of cubes needed
1	1
2	4
3	9
4	16
5	25

After recording 1, 4, 9 and 16 in the right-hand column, one child spotted an alternating odd/even pattern. More information was added to the results on the board:

Side length of square	Number of cubes needed	
1	1	
2	4	2 x what?
3	9	3 x what?
4	16	4 x what?
5	25	5 x what?

It was noted that the 'what' factor was the number in the first column which was the same as the first in the multiple. This enabled the children to predict larger squares and they prediced that a square with side length 6 would need 6 x 6 = 36 interlocking cubes. They tried this out and were delighted to confirm their prediction. Some children went on to try this for even larger squares.

We also looked at differences between the numbers in the second column:

$$4 - 1 = 3$$
$$9 - 4 = 5$$
$$16 - 9 = 7$$

David eagerly predicted. 'The next difference will be 9, and then 11 and then 13'. This was checked and agreed.

Further successful experience with investigating pattern in number encouraged the children to form predictions, to test these, then, in David's case, to move towards forming a generalization. He could not yet give the general case, but was able to use his knowledge of odd numbers to predict the next three cases.

The Triangular Numbers investigation was organized and then supported by the students. Their brief was for the children to make a series of steps using interlocking cubes and to record the number of cubes needed for each set (see figure 5.12). The results were recorded on the board, with all children having the opportunity to contribute. They produced the table shown in Figure 5.13.

The students informed me that some of the children's observations included the fact that the number of cubes for any flight of steps was the sum of the number of steps and the previous result, as indicated in Figure 5.13. This was something that was new to the students.

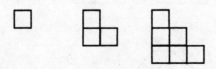

Figure 5.12 Triangular numbers, produced using squares

128

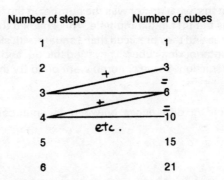

Number of steps	Number of cubes
1	1
2	3
3	6
4	10
5	15
6	21

Figure 5.13 Record produced by the children to record their observations about traingular number patterns

Student teachers reflect the same anxieties about mathematics as many classroom teachers. Many student teachers managed to obtain O-level or GCSE mathematics but without having enjoyed the subject. Many of them were taught through more didactic methods, where teachers illustrated the point and children then practised. This is very different from the method outlined by Caroline, where children are encouraged to investigate, to identify and use pattern, to travel on a voyage of discovery.

The Simple Tangram activity involved children in cutting out a simple tangram shape. They were set the task of making a rectangle, triangle, parallelogram and trapezium from the pieces (see Figure 5.14). This activity required much flipping and rotating of shapes and provided a challenging yet informal activity to consolidate and enhance earlier work on shape.

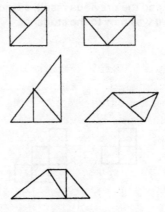

Figure 5.14 Simple tangram shapes

During the summer term, the children gradually developed their understanding of what was the same and what was different. The idea of shapes which were in reality the same only looking different because of their position, developed amongst most of the children. Conversations between children working together were most enlightening in portraying understanding and reasoning. It was particularly pleasing to see how many ideas from building shapes were retained and used in the similar pentominoes activity.

The activities which encouraged searches for number pattern resulted in many children independently searching for number pattern, even when this had not specifically been asked of them. All the children enjoyed the work: their level of commitment and concentration was evidence of that. Many of the less able pupils have achieved a good level of understanding. Not everyone achieved all that was asked of them, and some regarded the sharing of ideas as copying, cheating or stealing someone else's ideas. It was interesting to note which children preferred to work alone and which enjoyed working in conjunction with others.

The mathematics guidelines issued to schools in Scotland, SOED (1991), include the requirement that teachers plan activities which encourage pupils to:

learn to work independently and cooperatively in activities which involve explorations and problem-solving, calculating and measuring, and in applications to unfamiliar situations.

Children in Scotland are expected to show confidence, flexibility, invention and imagination, perseverance and to work systematically. In Caroline's class, some of the children demonstrated some of these qualities. Her description of committed, concentrating children shows how well she motivated them through the use of investigations which encouraged the children to use and apply their mathematical knowledge and to increase their understanding.

Children who have been used to working independently may well find the change to cooperative work quite difficult; different personal qualities are required. Children who have always worked on their own may feel that their work is their 'own', not to be shared with others. They may believe that to share ideas is wrong, that activities are competitive, that they must strive to do better than their peers. Such independent, competitive learning is often the result of using a commercial scheme, particularly one which is workbook- or workcard-based, where children can identify how well they are doing by how far through the scheme they have travelled. Desforges and Cockburn (1987) identify this as the children's race; teachers do not make public comparisons between children but the children still see the task as competitive. It is through working with others, through the stimulation of discussing ideas, through sharing thoughts about possibilities, that children can begin to be inventive and imaginative in their mathematics.

Caroline's children were beginning to understand what was involved in working through investigations and using problem-solving strategies; they had had little experience of working in this way before. Some of the children demonstrated that they were developing the skills and attitudes necessary to be successful, others would need more time and help before they felt confident to work both cooperatively and independently, depending upon what was asked of them. They were working towards developing the skills of recording their results in a clear and organized way (Ma1/3c), and were experiencing ways of designing data-recording sheets, (Ma5/2a), which will be essential skills for their further development of problem-solving skills.

CASE STUDY

4. Mathematical investigations, by Elizabeth Jones

How I wish that I had had the opportunity to learn through an investigational approach when I was a school child. For me, maths lessons were absolutely dreadful: I hated the subject, my understanding of concepts was poor, I was a low achiever in mathematics, I found no enjoyment in the study of the subject. I now look back on those years and realize why I was so poor at maths: I'm convinced that it was the way that I was taught. Nobody seemed to have any patience with me and very little was explained the second time around. In fact, if you were not a mathematical genius, the teachers did not want to know you. A sorry state of affairs, so much so that when I started my teaching career, I vowed that I would never, ever, teach maths to children the way I was taught. And that is still true today. Since undertaking a mathematics inservice course I have discovered the benefits of using mathematical investigations and made a firm commitment to introduce this approach into my classroom. The justification for using an investigational approach includes the following.

Mathematics should be enjoyed. It should be a means of communication and should support the mathematics that children will use in later life and particularly in their work. It should allow children to think logically and help them to have confidence in all that they do.

Providing a classroom atmosphere that is conducive to learning, being continuously aware of the child's previous work and assessing their knowledge and skills, are of paramount importance if the above aims and objectives are to be carried out. In addition to this, a variety of teaching methods are called for, linked to the size of the group of pupils.

The school where I teach progressively introduced a new mathematics scheme over the last two and half years. Included at the end of each topic section of the scheme are some investigations which the children enjoyed but which did not have enough depth to them for the child to become really absorbed in a worthwhile, meaningful investigation. I decided to introduce my own investigations to enhance this aspect of the children's work.

My class consisted of 26 Year 4 children, with an ability span from NC/SEAC Level 2 to Level 5. This ability range needed to be taken into account and carefully planned for. I decided to adjust my class timetable in order to allow a whole afternoon a week for this work. This would give the children the opportunity to work on an extended task, without the interruptions which occur if a short lesson time only is allowed.

Often children have too little time to complete an investigation which they have just started; this can be very frustrating. On the other hand, there are also occasions when it would be more appropriate to leave the task and come back to it at a later stage. Time away from the task, time for reflection upon what has been discovered, time to evaluate the procedures followed and observations made so far, can be helpful in identifying other avenues or strategies which could be useful. A combination of standard and longer lesson times would give children the opportunity to concentrate upon the task in hand, to reflect, to tackle extended tasks and to return to these tasks, as appropriate.

During the weeks when the mathematics investigations were underway, I learnt a lot about my children and about myself. I did not realize what changes would take place or for that matter would have to take place in order that my aims and objectives would be achieved. The whole afternoon per week did allow sufficient time. Although I did not realize it immediately, my role as teacher gradually changed during these sessions from one of responsibility for what the pupils do and learn to one of a resource for the pupils. From the start, my aim was not to give too much away to the pupils but to encourage the children to find answers or methods themselves. This I did by trying to answer their questions with another question which would evoke a response from them as opposed to a straightforward answer. Phrases such as:

Why do you think that?
What difference will that make?
Can you see a pattern?
Is it always so?
Is there another way of doing it?
Is there a better way?

were being used a lot more by myself, so much so that as the investigations continued, the children started to use the questions themselves whilst working. They began to take on more responsibility for the working out and tackling investigations for themselves, working either in pairs or in small groups. It was at this stage that I was able to relax more and listen to comments and observe how the work was being done. It was then that I became aware of just how efficient some of these children were becoming. What impressed me most of all was how they organized themselves to do their work. Provided they were given a set of guidelines at the beginning of the session, they could go on to cope with the situations presented to them. Another factor was the range of discussions that were going on while an investigation was in progress. The vocabulary, reasoning and thought-provoking ideas gave me endless pleasure to listen to and I really felt so proud of the children as they sounded so mature and sensible.

A calculator broken key investigation, *Cambridge Mathematics* (1991), allowed children to use just the 1 0 5 + = keys. They were asked to make 16, 37, 88 and 638, using as few keys as possible, and to record their results. Josie responded by showing a range of ways to make 16:

$15 + 1 = 16$ $\qquad$ $10 + 5 + 1 = 16$ $\qquad$ $5 + 5 + 5 + 1 = 16$
$10 + 10 - 5 + 1 = 16$

She had investigated a range of possible results before considering which one was the best fit. The last solution introduced subtraction, which was not within the original brief.

Stacie found:

$15 + 1 = 16$ $\qquad\qquad$ $5 + 10 + 1 = 16$
$5 + 5 + 5 + 1 = 16$ $\qquad\qquad$ $5 + 5 + 5 + 5 - 1 - 1 - 1 - 1 = 16$
$5 + 5 + 5 + 5 - 5 = 15 + 1 = 16$ $\quad$ $15 - 5 + 5 + 1 = 16$
$5 + 5 - 5 + 5 + 1 = 16$

She explored possibilities of addition and subtraction 'cancelling out'. Again, subtraction was used.

Lynette produced:

$5 + 5 + 5 + 1 = 16$

which became

$10 + 5 + 1 = 16$

and

$5 + 5 + 5 + 5 + 5 + 5 + 5 + 1 + 1 = 37$

which became

$10 + 10 + 10 + 5 + 1 + 1 = 37$

Lynette used the same method to find 88, first using combinations of 5s then of 10s. She did not try making a larger number as a starting point, such as:

$$55 + 10 + 10 + 10 + 1 + 1 + 1 = 88$$

However, Lynette used this approach in the next example:

$$510 + 105 + 10 + 10 + 1 + 1 + 1 = 638$$

The children demonstrated that they could explore the task and identify the problem, in as much as they all made the required number. However, none of them indicated where they had found the best solution, and both Josie and Stacey introduced subtraction, where only addition was to be used. The Scottish model for the process of problem solving and enquiry (SOED, 1991), encourages evaluation at all stages of the investigation (see figure 5.15). Through repeated evaluation of the task, children will be reminded of the problem and will check that their possible solutions or line of enquiry are within the framework of the task.

The children soon accepted these investigations as a challenge and as a consequence they became highly motivated, so much so that many asked if they could have more to do for homework. This gave me the opportunity to extend the investigations further and offered an ideal opportunity to

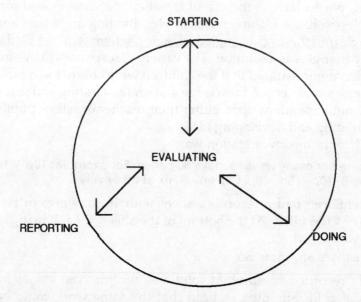

Figure 5.15 The Scottish model for the process of problem solving and enquiry (SOED, 1991)

involve the whole family. The reaction from the families was overwhelmingly positive – one father cancelled his swimming so that he could help his daughter. Frustration levels rose when hoped-for answers could not be achieved and one dad took the investigation to work. Never, ever, did I feel that I would have so much support and cooperation from parents. They were absolutely wonderful about the whole thing. I believed that the success of these home and class investigations was due to the fact that the children could put to use all their knowledge and understanding that they had already acquired in doing a task with which they felt comfortable and which was open to their own interpretation.

The first home investigation involved making acute angled triangles inside plane shapes. The children wrote some reminders to help them to work at home. These were:

right angle – 90°
shape
angles
tesellations
working with each other
thinking
reasoning

The children demonstrated that some were able to utilize the hints given, particularly in the use of tessellation. Some looked for the simplest solutions, thus, for example, dividing an obtuse angled triangle into three acute angled triangles, whereas others tiled with many triangles as a solution. The variety of responses to this investigation demonstrated that the children were able to use a range of strategies, a variety of knowledge and understanding and that they were not dependent upon either their teacher or fellow pupils for stimulating and developing ideas.

A later home investigation was:

There are many ways to make 50 pence. For example: 10p + 10p + 10p + 10p + 5p + 5p. Can you think of other ways?

The children had a recording sheet with 16 drawings of pots of money to be filled. At the bottom of the sheet, the following question was asked:

Are there any more ways?

Emily recorded 64 different solutions, writing coin values in the pots of gold. She then realized that the same work could be recorded by using arithmetic, such as:

8 x 5p + 10 x 1p

Her early solutions were random, in that one solution would contain a mixture of coins whilst the next contained one coin repeated, for example, 25 2p. However, her recording became much more systematic and she began to explore changing just one coin, thus:

    4 x 10p + 10 x 1p
    3 x 10p + 20 x 1p
    2 x 10p + 30 x 1p
    1 x 10p + 40 x 1p

The change in recording strategy from pots of money to arithmetical recording heralded the change in Emily's thinking. She saw a pattern which she could use to find a range of results, as shown above. She restricted variables and found that she could generate a pattern.

Sarah began by using the pots of money recording method. Like Emily, her results were random, one did not depend upon another. After she had filled her 16 pots, she set out her results in tabular form, using arithmetical notation. The following shows some of the patterns she generated:

    20p + 2 x 5p + 20 x 1p
    20p + 2 x 5p + 18 x 1p + 1 x 2p
    20p + 2 x 5p + 16 x 1p + 2 x 2p
    20p + 2 x 5p + 14 x 1p + 3 x 2p

and

    20p + 1 x 5p + 7 x 2p + 1 x 1p +1 x 10p
    20p + 1 x 5p + 6 x 2p + 3 x 1p +1 x 10p
    20p + 1 x 5p + 5 x 2p + 5 x 1p +1 x 10p

and

    2 x 10p + 1 x 5p + 7 x 1p + 9 x 2p
    2 x 10p + 1 x 5p + 9 x 1p + 8 x 2p
    2 x 10p + 1 x 5p + 11 x 1p + 7 x 2p

Possibly Peter could not cope with the possibility of more than 16 results and wrote 'No Man' against the question. Toby felt the same and wrote 'No way man!' Josie felt quite the opposite and wrote 'YES, Loads more' and proceeded to find them, too!

An issue raised by the children's responses is whether or not a given recording method will prevent some children from demonstrating that they can cope with the given task. The children who produced the more complete results for this work broke away from the suggested recording method and began to devise their own. This gave them the opportunity to explore pattern and led them to find a wide range of results in a systematic way. As the task had been set as a home investigation, others at home may well have influenced the recording of the work. But, in each case, the new method was adopted after using the given method and, in Emily's case, after many attempts with that method.

Perhaps both Emily and Sarah had identified the power of mathematical language and symbols to express their ideas. Haylock and Cockburn (1989) identify the connections between concrete experience, pictures, language and symbolic representation. Both children had moved from using a pictorial representation to a symbolic one; this proved a powerful tool as it allowed them to find more results in a structured way.

Some parents or guardians may find home investigations rather daunting, particularly if they had a poor experience of mathematics when they were at school. It is suggested that the home-school partnership must include support for parents if this venture is to be undertaken. Some adults may not be able to give adequate time to help their children during the week; giving a task in the middle or at the end of the week for the following week would allow parents a weekend in which to take part.

Some of the children who began the school year with me with learning difficulties developed a much more positive approach to their mathematics. They enjoyed working together or in small groups and asked if they could continue to work together and share ideas in all their maths lessons. I agreed to this and the results were very pleasing; their self-image improved tremendously; they are no longer hesitant; instead of a dislike for mathematics they are now more enthusiastic and enjoy their lessons more. Indeed, they were not the only ones to become more enthusiastic. Over the weeks I started to look forward and plan ahead for the investigational sessions, wondering what each one would bring. I noticed a gradual change in my approach to the class mathematics lesson in as much as I became very aware of question and answer techniques during those lessons. I also encouraged the children to question and reason out their answers more than they had done before.

I have been so pleased with this approach to teaching mathematics that I intend to bring it to the attention of other members of staff whom I feel sure would see the benefits just as I did. Finally, the children's reactions were tremendous and made the whole thing worthwhile. It is with them that I will leave the final comment.

Naomi: I enjoy the investigations very much. I like to take them home. Out of all the investigations I like the ones we take home. I prefer the ones we take home because we can involve our family.

Sarah: I enjoyed the homework very much it was fun to do. I liked the first investigation best because it was great fun to do and there were loads of ways to do it and when you were trying to find out if one way is right you find another. It was brilliant by the way. It was the money box investigation my mum and dad said it looked hard it was hard but it was really really fun. My sister joined in one of the investigations and she begged me to let her join in the rest!

Lynette: I have really enjoyed some of the investigations that I have been given even though they have been a bit hard. My favourite investigation that I have had is the investigation where you had to make up fifty pence out of different coins. I like that one best because it made me get my brain working and thinking what coins to put. It was also hard because you had to try and remember which ones I'd put so I didn't do the same one again. My mum and dad got annoyed when they couldn't work out what the answer was and then I came up with the answer.

John: My favourite investigation was the money because my mum was stuck on the investigation. But when my dad came in he did it and did the fifty pence one. Then my mum and dad had stuck on it but my sister got it. I was in the bath I near fell asleep but my mum clouted me so I got out quick and went downstairs.

Luke: I think the investigation sheets are good. I enjoyed taking them home, they made your brain rattle.

Toby: My favourite investigation was what acute triangle and I think it would be nice to do it again. I like doing investigations at home with mum and I like doing it at school with Peter.

For Elizabeth, the results of this work were most gratifying. She encouraged the children to develop a range of strategies for problem-solving and enquiry, which they then showed could be used at home in order to identify and solve problems. The children had developed positive attitudes towards mathematics, were prepared to persevere and to try different strategies. They demonstrated their knowledge of pattern in shape and number.

Planning strategies

Whatever planning method was used, whether a topic-focused planning method which involved other areas of the curriculum, a mathematics topic or planning for a process as in the last account, what is common to all four of these case studies is the detailed planning which the teachers undertook in order to ensure that the children would receive a rich, relevant mathematical diet.

It is possible from the above accounts to identify three separate planning strategies. A fourth one has also been adopted by some schools:

- using a cross-curricular theme or topic, where each area of the curriculum which is included is planned in detail, identifying relevant content from the programmes of study;

- using a mathematical topic, which brings together relevant content from the programmes of study of some or all of the mathematics attainment targets;
- using a published mathematics scheme;
- producing planning frameworks from programmes of study.

In the first two planning strategies, teachers need to understand the mathematical concepts implied in the programmes of study and feel confident to identify suitable activities to match that content. Two of the teachers who have contributed to this chapter refer to their anxiety about their competence to teach mathematics. One of them refers to children who are used to working independently through their published scheme which the school uses and who assess their success by the number of red ticks on a page.

In order to use a topic approach successfully, the mathematics included needs to be clearly identified, with account taken of development, continuity and progression. Two key questions need to be asked.

1. Does the chosen topic allow the appropriate level to be taught as new content?

Some topics naturally lend themselves to the development of particular concepts and skills. For example, Val Pendleton's topic of pattern was not only used across the curriculum, but also in subject teaching. She identified the pattern aspects of mathematics which were appropriate for the children to study. Jill Harmer, who also used pattern as her underlying theme, utilized other topics in order to teach this. Her's was a more integrated approach, using games as the basis for the children's work.

Graham (1991) raises the point that topics and themes usually consist of a series of related investigations or problems and that children only use mathematical thinking when the answers to specific questions are being sought. The dilemma for the teacher must be: can I devise activities within this topic framework which are mathematically challenging, which allow the children to learn new concepts and skills which arise naturally within the topic and which are also developmental?

Recent publications have included series of books to support the primary teacher in planning suitable content for topics. Examples of this can be found in *Themes Familiar* by Booth *et al.* (1987), which includes a wide range of themes with activity suggestions listed by subject area. The mathematics suggestions include problem-solving and investigations. However, the teacher's professional judgement is needed in order to make decisions about which activities would be suitable for the children's needs and to adapt other activities to ensure that they are suitable.

Part of the process of planning suitable content should include how this will be taught. How children are grouped, which aspects will lend themselves to group, individual or whole-class teaching, need to be considered. Will they be encouraged to use their investigatory and problem-solving skills? Will the development of mental methods be possible or appropriate in the given context?

2. Does the chosen topic allow children to use and apply concepts and skills which have already been introduced?

A topic may both lend itself to new mathematical concepts and be rich in opportunities for children to revisit concepts and skills already introduced. Particular lines of enquiry may be appropriate for one group of children whilst another group may follow a different track. A topic which allows children to revisit concepts and skills would offer the teacher opportunities to assess children's levels of attainment in those particular areas.

In considering both of the above key questions, it is important to consider the quality of the mathematical activities in which children will be engaged and to ensure that there will be suitable resource materials to provide support.

Many teachers will use a cross-curricular topic, choosing appropriate mathematics content, as well as a topic which is purely mathematical. These can be taught concurrently and are used in order to ensure that a balance is kept between learning new concepts and skills, using those already encountered and ensuring that skill with number is maintained.

None of the four teachers relied solely upon published mathematics schemes for their planning and teaching, but all four did use these in some way as a resource within their classroom. Those children who had been used to the 'loneliness of the long distance workbook' found problem-solving, cooperative and collaborative work more difficult to adjust to than those who had experienced working as a member of a collaborative group.

If teachers believe that there is pressure to teach mathematics as a single subject then one solution which they might adopt would be that of using a published scheme, which might be seen as having already done the planning. Most recently-published schemes offer a structured and sequential development approach to teaching and learning mathematics. However, these schemes need teachers to take responsibility for their use in the classroom and to make decisions about children's levels of attainment, children's learning needs, and appropriate teaching methods. This implies that teachers plan, identify suitable practical activities for children to begin to understand new concepts, and have a range of extension and reinforcement activities available. It does not imply that responsibility for successful learning of mathematics is handed over to the children or to the materials themselves.

Published schemes can provide structure and sequence for children's learning. However, teachers need to make decisions about what the next stage needs to be for each child. The ordering of specific mathematical topics and the need to revisit topics so that children's knowledge and understanding builds over time must be the teacher's responsibility.

Just ploughing through a scheme, as has happened in recent years with some of the workbook-based schemes, causes mathematics learning to become a competitive race between children. The risks of this approach include children rushing on ahead in the scheme, of not understanding and consolidating that misunderstanding. The latter can have serious repercussions, particularly when children have learnt how to jump through mathematical hoops without understanding how a process works, such as the decomposition algorithm for subtraction.

Another strategy that some schools have adopted is to identify relevant parts of the programmes of study of all the subjects on a term-by-term basis. Teachers are then free to choose whether to teach these through subject strands, topics or through both avenues. Again, to make this approach work, teachers need to understand the mathematics within the programme of study in order to be able to plan effectively and to choose appropriate activities. Such activities could be taken from published schemes, from mathematical or topic resource books.

Conclusion

As Alexander *et al.* (1992) point out, virtually no primary school works solely through topics. Most schools use a 'mix and match' approach, deciding which is more appropriate at a particular stage of development. A combination of topic approaches and published scheme can be used concurrently. However, whatever method of planning is used, it is important that the teacher understands the mathematical concepts, can identify suitable activities, and can also identify an appropriate developmental pathway for individual children.

Quality of mathematics teaching depends upon the teacher's understanding of the mathematics, rigorous planning for relevant content, and upon the method of delivery. Good quality mathematics teaching can come from a topic approach and from subject work; poor planning will lead to poor teaching in both approaches. Good quality planning and teaching require good quality resources for teachers and children, whether these be published schemes, resource books, or apparatus. Finally, teachers need the support of good quality inservice courses, so that their knowledge and understanding base and their confidence in teaching mathematics can be improved.

CHAPTER 6

The Management of Mathematics Teaching and Learning in Schools

This chapter considers the management of mathematics: who is responsible and how that responsibility is put into action. Case studies of three primary schools are considered in some detail. These were collected through observation and interview with mathematics coordinators, other teachers and headteachers. The fourth case study is from the head of mathematics of a high school, who discusses how all the schools in her area (the pyramid) have worked together to move towards some common understandings.

Successful mathematics teaching and learning is dependent upon five quality factors:

- the planning, teaching and evaluation cycle;
- the interactions between teachers and between teachers and children;
- the support given by the mathematics coordinator;
- the support given by the headteacher;
- the quality and availability of teaching materials.

How teachers have taken account of these quality factors in order to improve the learning opportunities for children is considered in detail.

The case studies are:

1. The newly appointed mathematics coordinator.
2. An informal approach to coordinating mathematics.
3. Planning effective learning from cross-curricular themes.
4. Liaison between primary and secondary schools.

CASE STUDY

1. The newly appointed mathematics coordinator, with a contribution from Graham S.

Graham had been appointed mathematics coordinator of a large, urban, 3 to 11 years, primary school. This was his second primary post. He had originally trained to teach secondary PE. The school was in an area of mixed housing, some owner occupied and some poor quality council housing. The majority of the children were white, others were Asian or African-Caribbean. The school's headteacher had been involved, through the LEA, with collecting materials for the PrIME Project (Shuard *et al.*, 1991) and was actively involved in primary mathematics development within the borough. She believed that active learning, which included investigations and problem-solving, encouraged good quality teaching and learning.

Graham had enrolled on a 20-day inservice mathematics course in order to update his knowledge and skills in mathematics and as coordinator. He reported that this gave him the opportunity to study the Mathematics National Curriculum in detail, to clarify his interpretation of the statements of attainment, to ensure that he had a common understanding with others taking the course. He spent some time working on mathematical investigations, increasing his understanding of the processes involved. What he had found particularly useful was the opportunity to work with other teachers who were also coordinators, to share experiences and anxieties, often over a cup of coffee. This had enabled him to extend his own knowledge and understanding of the mathematics curriculum and had raised his confidence in his ability to be effective in his role as coordinator. He had since started further inservice modules which would lead to a diploma in mathematical education. Graham felt that this experience, with the support of the specialist knowledge of the headteacher, would enable him to act as an agent of change of the mathematics curriculum of the school. Both the headteacher and Graham wanted to encourage a move towards investigations and problem-solving and to encourage a reduction in the amount of time spent by the children in drill and practice exercises. Graham was also expected to write a new mathematics policy. Why are these needed? What should they contain? Graham was required by his headteacher to write a policy; he had mixed feelings about what he had been asked to do. He stated:

I took up my post at Easter. By September, the headteacher wanted a new mathematics policy in place within the school. The school mathematics policy statement was based upon staff development meetings held before

I joined the staff. The head and I sifted through the minutes of the meetings and I agreed to help to write a statement based upon these minutes. My input to this process was minor, partly because I saw the headteacher as the expert and I deferred to her opinion, and partly because I had not been part of the discussion process. Since the staff discussions and the written document's production, there have been major changes to the staff, many of whom have been promoted to posts in other schools. Thus the document was based upon decisions taken by a minority of the present staff.

What, then, is the purpose of a written policy document? It is the framework which identifies a range of issues which need to be addressed in order that suitable teaching and learning approaches can be adopted. A policy takes time to be developed. It needs to be an agreed document, so that all members of staff have had the opportunity to make inputs to the discussion and that consensus has been reached. This can be an excellent opportunity for staff development, for the introduction of change in approach and style and for the identification of the need for curriculum and resource changes. It needs to include:

- a corporate statement, which has been agreed through discussion and is accessible to all staff;
- a clear basis from which to plan programmes of work;
- a statement which details children's entitlement to appropriate mathematical experiences;
- a framework for evaluating the effectiveness of mathematics teaching;
- clearly defined effective and efficient provision and use of resources;
- approaches to mathematics teaching, identification of effective styles of classroom organization and management;
- a coherent basis for identifying and meeting children's needs and capabilities;
- strategies for assessment;
- provision of quality resources.

The above framework can be used as a checklist when a new policy is being devised or when an existing one is re-examined. Most factors are common to all curriculum areas, for example, the identification of effective styles of classroom organization and management.

Graham's next task was to review the teaching materials currently in use in the light of the policy document which he had prepared.

Discussions with the headteacher suggested that the staff wanted freedom from a published scheme and that they were prepared to teach through a thematic approach. However, I felt it was important that I talked to individual members of staff and heard their views. I realized that what had been said at staff meetings did not necessarily represent the true views of individual teachers, who might not be willing to speak openly and who may have felt it necessary to concur with the headteacher's expressed wishes. I asked four questions:

What did you want from a scheme?
What were the present difficulties with the current scheme?
What would you like to be in place for September?
What would be useful to have in place for September?

I reported back to the headteacher. The staff had in the past concurred with the headteacher's wishes as they saw her as an expert, who must have the 'right' answers, whom they felt they must please, whereas they felt that they had no expert knowledge about mathematics. The head's view is, 'Maths is easy. Maths is all around you. All you have to do is reach out and grab it'. However, the staff were saying 'What we really need is some structure to our teaching.'

Graham's willingness to hold informal discussions with individual members of staff and, based upon this evidence, to counter the headteacher's view, increased the staff's trust in him, the headteacher's regard for his management skills and speeded the process towards a resolution for September.

It was agreed that a published mathematics scheme would give structure, support and stability to our teaching. It was also agreed that, if the staff were eventually to achieve what the headteacher wanted, that was, to work from themes, then using a carefully structured scheme would increase confidence and understanding so that the teachers would move towards taking control of their planning and teaching and become less reliant upon published schemes.

The staff and I drew up a short-list of published schemes which we found suitable, and I borrowed these from the LEA mathematics support team so that teachers could trial some of the materials in their own classrooms. By the end of the summer term the choice had been made of a new scheme which had explicit National Curriculum links. It was in place throughout the school for September.

During the first two terms of the implementation of the new mathematics scheme, no formal evaluation process was carried out. However, I continued to hold informal discussions with individual members of staff. It was found that the scheme had not included probability at Key Stage 1, which was felt by the staff to be a large omission. In order to overcome this, I wrote a package of materials, as part of my diploma course, for the infant department of the school, which the teachers trialled with their children. Towards the end of the third term of implementation it was agreed with the headteacher that a more formal approach to evaluation would be implemented during the following year.

As teachers' confidence grew with using the new scheme, there was an increased willingness to buy in other materials to use alongside the scheme to support, supplement and to extend the experiences for the children. I saw this as a positive step towards taking control away from the scheme and placing it with the teachers.

Two main threads can be seen in Graham's observations. These are:

- the high level of anxiety, insecurity and feeling of threat that the staff as a whole had about mathematics;
- the expressed need for an imposed structure upon the school's mathematics curriculum.

The first is easy to understand. The headteacher was known throughout the LEA as an expert on mathematical education. The majority of the staff were recent appointments; many of them had been appointed as probationers. Most of the more experienced staff had gained promotion out of the school. Thus there was an enthusiastic staff of mainly young teachers who did not have the knowledge or experience to draw the mathematical learning experiences from themes and topics. The Alexander *et al.* discussion paper, *Curriculum Organisation and Classroom Practice in Primary Schools,* (1992, ch. 5), contains detailed discussion of this issue and points to the poor quality of many instances of topic work. Many of the staff were unsure of their own mathematical understanding and of how to structure learning to ensure that the children learn in an effective manner. The headteacher's expertise was threatening; she was perceived to have a body of knowledge and understanding which was not shared by the rest of the staff. Her vision for the future was one that they were not yet ready to countenance.

The second point follows from the first. The need for security was very strong. This could be supplied by a carefully structured commercial scheme, which the whole school followed. This would give continuity and progression to the children's learning and act in some measure as staff development, as it would indicate one possible pathway through the knowledge, skills and understanding required of the National Curriculum.

This was a time of great pressure for Graham. He had one term in which to settle into a new school, gain the trust of his colleagues and arrange for a new curriculum to be in place for the start of the next term. The management strategies he used seem to have been successful. By informal discussions with individuals he encouraged an openness to grow. Staff became more willing to talk about their perceptions of their own inadequacies. Graham, in return, offered the opportunity to put in place something that would offer support, structure, continuity and progression. He opened up channels of communication between himself and the other staff members, which, if nurtured, would allow for continued support and curriculum development.

What was needed next was a structure for evaluating the effectiveness of the new scheme. The informal evaluation which Graham carried out through continued discussion with individuals identified some shortfalls of the scheme and of school resources. However, the effectiveness of the scheme as a stimulus for the children, what they learnt and how effectively, what the scheme did well, what the staff found difficult – none of this was considered, unless particular points were raised during informal discussions. Graham felt that to use a formal staff meeting to discuss the scheme would be counter-productive as he believed that the staff were not yet confident enough in their own mathematical ability to discuss their work in a formal setting. However, it would have been useful to ask groups of staff who taught within the same year or key stage, to begin the process of formal evaluation, using agreed criteria.

The informal evaluation which Graham initiated produced other opportunities for development.

In introducing the new scheme it became apparent that there was a shortage of suitable classroom equipment for practical work. This was particularly apparent for capacity and weight. The resources for measures were stored centrally as it was school policy to teach these as a topic. However, I wanted other mathematics resources moved out of cupboards, where they were languishing, into classrooms, so that they would be available for practical experiences for the children.

The staff knew how much money was available each year for resources. It was part of my role as coordinator to reach a consensus on how the money allocated to mathematics would be spent. I insisted that priority must be given to the reception classes' needs, as I believe that this would provide a firm foundation upon which the rest of the school could build in later years. Another priority which I set for myself was to find suitable investigative materials to supplement what was already happening. This was an area which I felt needed support throughout the school.

Through informal evaluation of the implementation of the new scheme, the need to formulate a policy for resources had arisen. Most resources were placed in year bases, so that those teachers had immediate access to the resources which were deemed necessary for their teaching. Staff had received a list of which items had been placed in which year base and what was held centrally by me. Items borrowed from the central store or from a year base other than a teacher's own were recorded on a loan list, so that it was possible to identify who had which items in their classroom. This worked effectively.

Why do resources so often lie unused in cupboards? There are two main reasons for this.

1. What is available in the resource area is not known to staff. As Winteridge (1989) states, part of the responsibilities of a mathematics coordinator should be to ensure that resources are readily available, perhaps through carefully labelled boxes or drawers, through a resources list for each member of staff, or through a booking-out system, so that it is possible to identify who has borrowed what and when.

2. Staff do not know how to or do not feel confident to use the resources. A typical example of this would be the boxes of coloured, graded wooden rods which used to be used for developing number bonds. These have been rediscovered by some schools and are now being used for exciting algebra work. Coordinators can run workshop sessions for staff, when resources which are not being used can be demonstrated. This can be particularly effective, if the resources are used in activities which staff can then try within their classrooms. New resources need to be displayed so that all staff know that they are available. A short workshop session to demonstrate how to use them and ideas for using them will increase the confidence of staff.

A structured approach to the introduction of new resources and support for using existing resources can help to build the confidence of teachers who feel unsure about moving towards a more practical approach to mathematics teaching.

Staff development for mathematics had a low priority as there had been a considerable input before my appointment and the implementation of the new scheme appeared to be progressing successfully. The school priorities were history, geography, art, music and physical education. I believe that informal discussion with staff is an effective means of communication and that I was able to help and advise more effectively in this informal setting than in a large staff meeting. I needed more time to develop my own skills as a mathematics educator before leading staff inservice sessions.

Graham had worked as mathematics coordinator for nearly four terms when he was interviewed. He summed up his experience within the school as follows.

I have street cred with the staff. This comes from my diploma course, because I have some understanding of the shape of the mathematics National Curriculum. I have had considerable experience in dealing with people: the head, staff and parents. I'm sure all of this gives confidence to the staff to put their point of view. I have aimed to increase the staff's trust in me, to raise their confidence level, to facilitate the development of mathematics in the school. My aim for the future? IT. This is an area within the school which I would like to see developed.

In order for an innovation to be successful, a range of factors come into play to ensure effective implementation, as discussed in Day *et al.* (1985):

- teachers need to see the need for change and to feel a shared responsibility for implementation;
- the need for staff cooperation. Paying lip-service to the need for change will not be effective. All teachers will need to agree on a programme of implementation and to show that they have played their part;
- good, clear communication. This will help everyone involved to hear the same message and to understand its implications. It will enable feedback between staff to be an effective means of identifying the strengths and weaknesses of the project and to allow for re-planning as time goes on;
- positive support from the headteacher. The headteacher is able to support through positive feedback to all those involved, through the provision of necessary resources, through ensuring that positive messages about the development are received by parents and governors;
- positive support from the mathematics coordinator. The coordinator has the subject expertise, understands the processes involved and has a vision of the benefits to the children's learning which will follow. Practical, positive support, listening and advising, will help others to maintain their feelings of responsibility and to continue to strive for success. Support and encouragement will boost morale;
- time. Time to implement; time to monitor and evaluate; time to assimilate the implications, so that teachers feel ownership of each stage of the process in which they have agreed to be involved. Graham found that there is a need for one change at a time, so that one success can lead to another, rather than being swamped by too many considerations;
- identification of the personal benefits of the proposal as well

as those to the school as a whole. 'What is in this for me?' is a question that each teacher will ask. A satisfactory answer will be required before teachers devote time and energy to any innovation.

Successful innovation, whether of the school policy document, of the use of new materials, or of the introduction of new curriculum, creates a feeling of belonging amongst staff. They have all shared in the same adventure, which has had a good outcome. Once there has been time for evaluation and assimilation, the next project may be easier to introduce.

One of Graham's major achievements was his ability to build strong relationships with the staff and to help them to feel part of the development process. This increased confidence amongst all of those teachers who had felt insecure. Graham would need to continue with this high level of support for some time. Compare his success with that of Denise at another primary school, within the same LEA.

CASE STUDY

2. An informal approach to coordinating mathematics, with a contribution from Denise A.

The 3 to 11 year primary school where Denise was coordinator for mathematics was formed by the amalgamation of the infant and junior schools, in 1984. The two schools had shared the same campus, with adjoining buildings which were linked by a common entrance. The majority of the children were Asian, most were second generation, with English as their second language, whilst a significant minority were first generation who spoke no English on entry to school. Other children were from African-Carribean, Arab and local white families. Eight years after the amalgamation there was still reference to 'the infants department...the junior department', as though they were separate schools with separate identities. Denise had been mathematics coordinator for about five years. She found that many of the staff lacked confidence in their mathematical ability and consequently in their teaching. This discouraged change, the introduction of new initiatives. She found her role as coordinator quite difficult because, 'Maths is a subject where teachers don't like it, don't want to do it.'

Five years ago, there was no agreement amongst the staff about mathematics teaching. Each member of staff had developed their own curriculum. There was no coordination, no collaboration, no attempt at continuity and progression for the children. In view of the undercurrent of insecurity about mathematics, it was decided by the whole staff to adopt a published mathematics scheme. The one chosen was workcard-based for the younger children and textbook-led for the juniors. For the staff, this offered a set route through the mathematics curriculum. In the front of each child's mathematics exercise book the teacher stuck a sheet which listed the modules to be covered at that stage and the order in which they were to be done. As these were completed, the teacher ticked them off. This was revised for Key Stage 1 following the introduction of the mathematics National Curriculum. Understanding of place value concepts was included in the scheme for the infant classes, rather than, as before, leaving this to the junior department to teach. This had been a sensible decision, particularly with the rapid development the children in Years 1 and 2 had made with large numbers through their use of Logo (see Chapter 3.)

I carried out the development of the route through the scheme and other staff agreed to my suggested route. Some five years after the introduction of the use of a published scheme the uncertainty about mathematics teaching is still evident.

Why was there still so much uncertainty? The school staff fell into two distinct groups: those who had been at the school for many years and those who were recent appointments, mainly probationers or second-post appointments. Past experience suggested that recently appointed staff would not stay at the school for more than four or five years before accepting promotion to another school. Thus, there was a sizeable group of teachers who had not been part of the original planning which had led to the adoption of the published scheme and had not received the support of more formal sessions to review its effectiveness. With the rapid introduction of the National Curriculum, the staff had needed to review each curriculum subject as the documentation became available. Time for mathematics workshop sessions, which could have helped to increase confidence amongst the staff, had not been available. Denise found herself supporting staff who had a wide range of experiences in teaching mathematics. As the Mathematical Association (1988) advises, the task for Denise is to challenge strengths whilst minimizing weaknesses.

With the introduction of the National Curriculum, it had been necessary to carry out an audit of the published scheme, to identify its strengths and weaknesses. I carried this out in isolation, reporting my findings back to the senior management team (headteacher, deputy, curriculum coordinators and year heads who hold a C allowance). Supplementary material had been purchased, including some calculator investigation material. This had been identified through the success of the PLUM project with the younger children (see Chapter 3). Materials to support the juniors for calculator work were provided.

As mathematics coordinator, I am responsible for all mathematics resources. I ascertain what is needed through discussions with individual members of staff; needs are then prioritized by me. The published scheme needs replenishing on a yearly basis. Supplementary materials have assumed a higher priority because of the requirements of the National Curriculum.

Denise, like Graham, had used the informal approach, had talked to individual members of staff to obtain feedback about the effectiveness of what had been put in place and to ascertain resource needs. However, a more formal, structured approach had not been available, due to the pressure of National Curriculum implementation. Much of the decision-making about resources was left to Denise. It depended upon her view, her priorities. This system of informal discussions followed by Denise making decisions had not helped to reduce the high level of insecurity about mathematics amongst the staff.

Some basic resources, such as Multilink or Unifix cubes, are stored in classrooms. All other resources are kept in a central storage area for mathematics and teachers and children can borrow from the central resource as the need arises. However, no records are kept of what has been borrowed by whom, so that there are occasions when items are missing and nobody admits to having them in their classroom. I store the spare textbooks for the junior classes in my classroom. The children come, with pride, to request the next book. It gives me the opportunity to discuss their work and progress with individual children.

Children who have access to resources on a needs basis will also be able to act independently of their teacher. The children were encouraged to increase their level of autonomy through taking responsibility for collecting and returning resource materials. A simple system of checking who has which resources can be introduced which children from reception onwards can operate. If every item or collection of resources has a clearly identified 'home', what is borrowed can be replaced by a card with the class name on it. When the resources are returned, the card is removed.

The value of keeping spare textbooks in a teaching room is to be questioned. Observation showed that every day there were five or six interruptions from children who needed the next book. Whilst the value of discussing a child's achievement is not dismissed, it is difficult to see how this can be carried out effectively within another class's teaching time.

> On classroom wall displays, numbers, days of the week and months of the year are in English and Gujerati. During their mathematics work, as in other curriculum areas, children sometimes converse in their home language. Children who have only recently come to Britain will have their teacher's explanations translated for them by a friend.

All children were valued. It was interesting to note that during some 30 visits to the playground no evidence was found of racial abuse. The children had been encouraged by the school to value their culture, traditions and language. Dual language books were available in all classrooms. Traditional Islamic patterns had been used as starting points for investigations. This was a happy and caring school but one that had still to resolve issues with regard to the levels of confidence shown by the staff in mathematics.

CASE STUDY

3. Planning effective learning from cross-curricular themes, with a contribution from Jenny D.

Jenny is headteacher of a two teacher village school in a rural county in the south-west of England. She had been there for a year when the following interview was conducted. The school building is tiny. Jenny teaches the older children, 20 of them, aged 7 to 11. The other teacher, in her second year of teaching, has the 5 to 7 year-olds in a mobile classroom in the playground.

> No published scheme is used. We meet regularly to plan. Our starting points are the children's interests, rather than the National Curriculum attainment targets and statements of attainment. We find that from the work which we plan, it is possible to identify which areas of the National Curriculum would be covered. Very careful planning records are kept so that we are able to check during the course of each year that there are no curriculum gaps. The areas of interest which the teachers or the children identify to be explored are across the curriculum. Mathematics is taught in two ways: as part of a topic, which is particularly used for children to use and apply their mathematical knowledge and understanding and as a subject in its own right, with particular concepts or skills identified for development. As the need for new mathematics arises, perhaps within a cross-curricular topic, we teach that concept.

In this case study, Jenny acted as mathematics coordinator. The

154

second teacher was recently qualified; she relied upon the expertise of Jenny to support her in her planning and teaching. Jenny had previously been deputy head of a large London primary school, which had used a similar method for planning to the one she adopted here. In order for this method of planning to be successful, there must be trust and respect between those involved. There also needs to be a clear policy statement which sets guidelines for planning for quality teaching and learning.

> The children in my class are studying the topic of flight. We start each session with a planning meeting, during which it is agreed what task each child will carry out. One group chose to investigate making parachutes and testing them. Within this activity, the children were involved in designing and making the parachutes, (technology), identifying suitable materials and testing them, (science), measuring the amounts of material to use, measuring the length of the parachute strings, making decisions about the shape of the flat material for the parachute canopy, and making accurate timings of the parachutes descending (mathematics). The activity was started yesterday, and was not completed today. The children chose which group to work with, and the groups are of mixed age, mixed ability and both boys and girls. The children talk to each other about their work. During the hour which they spent on the task they made and tried three different parachutes. I observed what they had done and asked open questions during the session. Before the end of the morning, the whole class came together and each group chose a representative to report back to the class. Other children were encouraged to ask questions. The childen are encouraged to praise each others' efforts.

During the same session two children made a hardback book for a report they had written. Again, the activity was cross-curricular. They needed to make careful and accurate measurements to cut card and decorative paper. The finished result was quite beautiful and made very carefully and accurately.

> Around the walls of the classroom, I have set up some interactive displays. These include mathematical puzzles and investigations. When a child completes one of these they are encouraged to leave a message for another child, perhaps leaving their solution and challenging others to find a different one. I have covered table tops and cupboard tops with lengths of fabric with tessellating patterns on them. Each time a child finishes a story or project they are encouraged to make it into a book, which is displayed for others to enjoy. I try to ensure that the classroom environment is attractive as well as functional.

Published materials were available as a resource for both the children and the teachers to use. However, these were considered secondary to the children's needs. Much of the curriculum material was purpose-made by the teachers and consisted of worksheets, workcards and games.

This is a very different approach from those of Graham and Denise. The children were eager to work at the tasks which had been set. They appeared to be mature, sensible in their attitudes towards each other, able to work collaboratively, and valued each other's opinions. As this approach to the curriculum was common in all subject areas, the children had quickly become used to working in this way. However, this approach needs the control of a coordinator who has confidence in her or his mathematical ability and who can help and support others so that they share this confidence. There needs to be:

- the agreement of all the staff that they would wish to plan and teach through topics and without the use of a structured scheme. If lip-service only is paid, then the innovation will fail as there will be no commitment to its success;
- a clear structure within which topics are planned. The advice contained within the Non-Statutory Guidance (NCC, 1989, section F), identifies a rationale for teaching in this way and indicates issues which need to be taken into account in planning;
- careful monitoring of what is to be taught in order to ensure that 'gaps' in conceptual development or in subject content are identified. The National Curriculum Programmes of Study contain the detail of what must be taught. Many schools have adopted a simple system of grids which identify ATs and SOAs and how frequently these have been visited by the children. Such a system will also identify the gaps;
- inclusion of any 'gaps' that are identified in subesquent planning. Care needs to be taken that artificially contrived topics are not invented in order to cover gaps. Teachers might consider that if particular mathematics topics do not fit comfortably within a theme, then it is appropriate to teach these as a mathematics topic in their own right;
- a record-keeping system which identifies not only what children have covered but also what they have learned (see Chapter 7 for further discussions of this);
- a monitoring and evaluation process which is used to feed forward in the planning cycle. Evaluation is needed of what was successful and why, and of what needs modification and how

that can be achieved. Honesty by the whole staff is required to make this process effective;

- a quality resource bank of ideas and activities, which can be referred to both for initial planning and for individual activities as needs arise. If a cross-curricular approach to planning and teaching is to be adopted, then the resources which were already in use will contain many ideas, activities, investigations and practice items, which will be of use in planning. An effective monitoring and evaluation process will aid the identification of resource needs.

The planning, teaching and evaluation cycle

The staff need to be involved from the beginning of the planning cycle, especially when such fundamentally important issues as the introduction of new teaching materials are concerned. A review of what is already in use needs to be undertaken and materials which are under consideration checked against stated needs and the school policy statement. If an effective monitoring and evaluation programme is in place, then it is possible to identify strengths and weaknesses of such an innovation during its first run through. Any weaknesses can be dealt with so that the children's entitlement to a broad and balanced curriculum is not affected. Teachers need to know that there is continuity and progression within each class and throughout the school so that the teaching and learning which they undertake with their class can be seen to be pertinent to the children's learning at subsequent stages.

The interactions between teachers and between teachers and children

Discussions with colleagues at an informal level, over a cup of coffee, whilst comparing notes during lunchtime and after school, can be both reassuring and supportive. The opportunity to share experiences – what is working well, what is more difficult – encourages mutual trust and support and can encourage teachers to work together to seek possible solutions. However, what is identified within such informal discussions can be sufficently important to need a wider audience. During the introductory stages of the implementation of change it is helpful to hold regular meetings to share successes and to discuss issues which have arisen.

A school policy statement which requires small-group work,

with children encouraged to collaborate and to take responsibility for their own learning for much of the day, needs to be supported with suitable staff development.

The support given by the mathematics coordinator

In the above three case studies, Graham, Denise and Jenny (who was also the headteacher), held discussions with the staff on an informal basis to identify what help and support was required. For the implementation of, for example, a new scheme to be success-ful, the mathematics coordinator must offer praise, help and be willing to listen. Teachers need praise for the good work done, for the suggestions for improvement and for being willing to trial something new. The coordinator must be willing to listen to comments about the strengths and the weaknesses of the innova-tion. This will enable the coordinator to offer help so that what has proven to be unsuccessful, not understood or difficult to organize and manage, can become successful, understood and manage-able.

The following four awarenesses, identified by Whitaker (1984) need to be developed by mathematics coordinators in order to aid identification of the factors which will aid or inhibit staff develop-ment.

a. How individual teachers behave. Who is able to ask for help, who needs to be reassured, who will be willing to contribute new ideas, who feels threatened by change. An analysis of such factors will aid identification of who will offer support and who will need to be sup-ported, when change is considered.
b. Where the sources of power lie and how they operate. There are two sources to be considered: the official, which operates through the headteacher and senior management team; the unofficial, which may not be applicable in smaller primary schools, which is who 'has the ear' of the headteacher and the senior management team, whose opinion is sought out and listened to. If an unofficial power source operates in a school, then it will be necessary to ensure that the wielder of this power is sympathetic to what is being proposed.
c. The values system of the school. Again, there may be two sets of values: those that are openly stated and those that form part of the hidden agenda of a school.
d. How the proposed change will affect each of these factors. Who will be threatened by the proposal? Who is likely to respond positively

and act as an ally? Will other curriculum areas be affected and who coordinates those? What are the resource implications and will these have a major or minor affect upon the school capitation budget?

A successful mathematics coordinator is one who is receptive to other teachers' ideas; realizes that other people will make mistakes; is tolerant of the failings of others; and exercises powers of self-restraint. Indeed, not a paragon, but a teacher who respects the feelings of others and recognizes that being a coordinator does not make you infallible.

The support given by the headteacher

The role of the headteacher is to lead, to encourage, to support, to provide resources in all areas of the curriculum to enable the teaching and learning process to be successful. Where a school has a mathematics coordinator, the headteacher will have delegated part of that role. Where there is no coordinator, as in Jenny's case, the head will have assumed that role. The need for discussion and for consensus, before the introduction of new materials, is paramount. Otherwise, difficulties will arise, as teachers who are not consulted will feel that they are not valued.

The quality and availability of teaching materials

The availability of quality teaching materials can be a central issue in achieving quality teaching and learning, particularly with so many pressures upon classroom time from an overloaded primary curriculum. Where quality materials are readily available and teachers have been encouraged to use these for planning and teaching, then there will be clear benefits for the children and their learning. These benefits are of two kinds. First, where published resources and teacher-produced materials have been collected, these can offer help and support for teachers for planning quality learning activities for the children. Second, where thought has been given to the types of equipment and structured apparatus for the children to use to support their learning, then there will be awareness amongst the teachers of the suitability of particular materials for particular tasks. For example, interlocking cubes can be used to help children to understand 'take away' subtraction, as the linked cubes can be broken down to make different representations of quantities. Coloured rods, which have a numerical value, can be helpful when children compare quantities for 'difference' subtraction. A clear policy which states who is responsible for resources needs to be in place and to be seen to be working. The implementation of such a policy would normally be the responsibility of the mathematics coordinator. If all members of staff have been consulted on decisions to be taken about new purchases, storage, access to materials, then systems set in place for the organization and management of resources will be more likely to succeed.

In schools where teachers' professionalism has been acknowledged and their opinions and expertise valued, it is possible for there to be open exchanges in discussions, for staff to work together, for all to take part in decision-making, so that there is a sense of ownership of changes in curriculum and classroom management.

In many localities, teachers have identified positive collaboration between schools as a means to improve learning opportunities for children. Management of mathematics teaching and learning across the divide between primary and secondary schools is necessary in order to encourage continuity and progression. In the following case study, the head of mathematics in a secondary school describes how little effective collaboration there had been and what measures were taken to improve collaboration across the pyramid.

4. Liaison between primary and secondary schools, with a contribution from Janet C.

Janet had been head of mathematics in the only secondary school in a rural area for two years. One of her concerns on taking up her post was how to encourage effective collaboration between high school and the feeder primary schools. The pyramid of schools consists of one large town junior school, one large town infant school, and eight village primary schools, some of which had just 30 pupils. The heads of all the schools agreed that there would be, every term, a meeting for the coordinators of each subject. Janet described what had happened.

> When I first started at the high school, the secondary staff were told that they had to go to all the pyramid meetings. The head of the high school or the deputy would also be present to take the minutes. If we were lucky, there would be a maximum of three teachers from the other primary schools, five of us secondary maths teachers and our head or deputy. What was

happpening was that the secondary school was dictating that there would be all these curriculum meetings for all the subjects and whereas there were different staff from the high school attending each one, for the small primary schools it was the same member of staff trying to attend a meeting for a different subject every week. So they were overloaded and to cope, teachers were cutting out some of the pyramid meetings, probably because the agenda for the meetings was set by the secondary school.

One of the first things I tried was to make the meetings have a stronger primary focus, such as suggesting that the next meeting could be to discuss maths at, say, Key Stage 1. Another thing that I did, soon after I started at the school, was to visit each of the primary schools, to get to know the teachers and to increase my understanding of what the teachers were achieving. We were getting complaints that, as a secondary school, we took no notice of what the primary schools had achieved. I saw that there were many good mathematical things going on in the primary schools. This also gave me the opportunity to ask the teachers what they would find useful to discuss at the meetings, rather than us dictate to them what would be discussed.

This worked to a certain extent but the primary teachers still were not happy because the meetings were being held at the secondary school and the head or a deputy was always present. We've managed to change that now so that I take the responsibility of minuting the meetings and the head or a deputy no longer attends. All the schools take it in turns to host the meetings. That's made a really big change. It seemed as though we weren't trusted before, or, at least, that's how the teachers saw it. Then it was a matter of finding topics that teachers would be interested in.

Historically, the first meeting of each year has been to discuss the placements or the setting of each pupil who has transferred to us. Only one of the primary schools, the town junior, was interested in this and it could become quite argumentative. As we based our setting on the feeder schools records it has become clear that the way in which the agreed records are filled in needs to be agreed across the curriculum.

We have had some very successful meetings. At one meeting, the infant teachers talked about the National Curriculum and what this had meant for them in terms of planning, assessing and record-keeping. This was very useful as it indicated to the junior and secondary teachers what we were going to be faced with. The infant teachers enjoyed having the floor, being able to put across to others their point of view and having the realization that their contribution was a most valued one.

The change in the format of the meetings led to a gradual increase in the number of teachers attending. I offered to run a Use of Calculators from 5 to 16 session when it was the turn of one of the small village schools to act as host. Now, although every school had calculators, their use of them was very limited and I hoped to encourage the teachers to use these more with their pupils. Sixteen teachers attended this meeting. There were three secondary teachers and the rest were primary teachers; some teachers had brought teacher friends along. I think that they thoroughly enjoyed it. I had aimed the content towards the younger age group and used ideas which could be adapted for different age groups and for a range of skills which teachers would want their pupils to practise.

Another very successful meeting was held, this time at the high school as we could provide a computer room. Each teacher brought some computer software which they had found successful. Each teacher showed their software and talked about how they used it in the classroom. We were surprised to find that there was very little repetition in what was shown. The primary teachers enjoyed this as it gave them the opportunity to see a range of software which was new to them.

One of the major benefits of the pyramid working together has been the build-up of trust between us; and honesty: now we find that we can say what we need to say, for instance, 'We don't seem to be doing this very well; what do you do?', whereas before no one would say anything. We have offered to loan equipment to the primary schools and they borrow items of equipment which they can't afford for a week or two weeks. Science has started to do this as well. Some teachers are beginning to talk about the fact that they don't know how to teach some topics because they're not maths specialists. This encourages the sharing of ideas and suggestions without being threatening. It's taken two years to get this far.

Where do we go from here? Well, something that I should like to see us develop is a maths dictionary across all ages and abilities. This is for pupils to develop their own definitions, in their own words. I think both children and teachers will enjoy developing this. One of the things I have learnt is how good particularly the infant teachers are at communication with their pupils. Their use of language is far superior to mine. I have a great admiration for their skills in this area and have learnt a lot from observing in their classrooms. I believe that language development is one of the strengths of the Key Stage 1 teachers. I believe that if we develop the maths dictionary this will enable them to use their strengths and that they won't feel so threatened by maths. It will also mean that some of the language which the pupils still find hard when they come to us at 11 can have been introduced in a much more relaxed way. Words like 'multiplication' and 'division' (they only know times and share!) could become part of all the pupils' vocabulary at the primary stage. Another topic that every one wants to look at is mental mathematics. This is something that we want to encourage across the pyramid, to be developed on a regular basis.

It is very hard to set an agenda for our meetings. The primary teachers do not like a formalized agenda. If anything too formal, too mathematical, is planned for a meeting, then many of the primary teachers don't turn up. They can opt out. This is divisive and not taken well by the secondary staff who are told that, whatever the item to be discussed, they have to attend the meetings as part of directed time. I think all of us could do with just sitting down over a cup of coffee and chatting. But at the end of the day, I have to write up the minutes of the meeting, of what was discussed and why and submit them in triplicate to my school's directorate. I don't get any feedback from these. Copies are sent to all the headteachers of the primary schools. I have to say how impressed I have been by the professional attitude of my primary colleagues. Everything that they do is for the best interests of the pupils. They take both long-term and short-term views into account.

162

The beginnings of cross-phase collaboration are rooted in a growing understanding of what each sector does and does well. These beginning stages show how difficult non-specialist teachers can find mathematical ideas. The realization comes that secondary schools and primary schools need to cooperate, to share their perspectives, so that they can build towards continuity, in order to provide a rich mathematical curriculum for all their children, and with this will come, as Bell and Day (1991) state, the need to monitor, to evaluate, to analyse, across all key stages, in order to provide an effective, worthwhile teaching and learning environment.

Conclusion

In this chapter, the role of mathematics coordinator was considered. The successful coordinator will lead new initiatives, identify needs, listen, support and encourage. With the implementation of the National Curriculum, most publishers have seized the opportunity to issue either new schemes or revisions of existing ones, or to produce other published materials to support the teaching of mathematics topics such as probability or algebra. The coordinator will need to act effectively in supporting all the staff as decisions are made about the need for resources. However, it is evident that there is also need for liaison across the primary/secondary divide in order for both sectors to provide for effective teaching and learning.

CHAPTER 7

Assessment and Record-keeping

This chapter considers the two aspects of the National Curriculum which have been the most contentious. These are teacher assessment of children's attainment and the records which need to be kept for forward planning and reporting purposes. Lack of confidence in assessment and its associated procedures was expressed privately, which is the main reason that most contributors to the chapter asked to remain anonymous. Evidence from contributors was obtained through interview between them and the author and, in one case, through collection of records from the teacher's record books. The chapter is in two sections:

Assessment through interaction between child and teacher.
This contains the following case studies:
1. Sorting activity involving weighing with Year 1 children.
2. Weighing task with Year 2 children.
3. Unplanned teacher assessment. (This draws upon case studies from other chapters).

Record-keeping
This contains the following case studies:
4. Record-keeping at two schools from the same LEA.
5. Gathering evidence of attainment.
6. Transfer records.

Assessment through interaction between child and teacher

Teacher assessment involves both active and passive forms of observation by the teacher of the child. Teacher assessment can be achieved through observation by the teacher of the child, discussion between child and teacher, or a discussion between children which is overheard by the teacher. It can involve observations and discussions about children's recording of their work. HMI (1991) reports that good practice involves the use of a range of assessment techniques: observation, questioning, discussion and marking. These techniques may be specifically planned to obtain evidence of attainment or they may be used spontaneously.

This first part of this section contains case histories from teachers who planned to collect evidence for assessment of Ma1. This attainment target contains the three strands of application: mathematical communication and reasoning, logic and proof. Opportunities to assess children's progress in this attainment target are very frequent because it is the attainment target which pervades the children's mathematical activity. Whilst assessing attainment for Ma1, evidence for other attainment targets will also be gathered, as Ma1 forms the framework within which children acquire the knowledge, skills and understanding from the programmes of study for number, algebra, shape and space, measures and handling data. Such evidence needs to be gathered over time, so that Ma1 evidence can be gained in a variety of contexts. It is unlikely that any one activity will provide evidence for all aspects of Ma1 assessment. HMI (1991) report that teachers found the assessment of attainment of Ma1 more difficult than for the other attainment targets. They attribute this to lack of previous experience as using and applying mathematics previously received little attention. In the second part of this section, unplanned teacher assessment is considered and examples have been taken from teachers' observations in Chapters 3 and 4.

CASE STUDY

1. Sorting activity involving weighing with Year 1 children

The children in my class are used to working in groups for discussion about mathematics. I use these sessions for developing the children's thinking and communication skills and for assessing their attainment so that suitable activities can be planned for the future. On the occasion I describe below, some of the Y1 children were to work with me on an individual basis. The activity was a sorting activity, which required the children to make decisions about heavier and lighter objects when compared with a standard. I was careful to change details of the approach to avoid other children repeating responses that they had heard from others.

Ifor and Mariam were assessed individually. I worked with each child in a quiet area of the classroom. There was a box with an assortment of objects and two plastic set rings. We talked.

Teacher: I've got some different things in this box and I'd like you to sort them out for me. Let's take this. What is it?

Ifor:	A tennis ball.
Teacher:	Yes. Would you like to pick out something else?
	[Ifor chose a plastic bottle.]
Teacher:	Can you tell me which is heavier, the ball or the bottle?
	[Ifor held one in each hand and compared them.]
Ifor:	The ball.
Teacher:	Put the ball in one of the set rings then, where we will keep all the things which are heavier than the bottle. Now, take something else out of the box and see if it is heavier or lighter than the bottle.

Ifor compared by holding to find which items were heavier and which were lighter than the bottle, putting the heavier in one set ring and the lighter in the other. He took a pebble from the box and then had difficulty in making a decision.

Teacher:	What have you got now?
Ifor:	A stone. What shall I do? They both feel the same.
Teacher:	Can't you decide which is heavier?
Ifor:	This...no, this.
Teacher:	How can you be sure?
Ifor:	Use the balance.
Teacher:	Can you get one then and find out?

He selected a simple balance from the table where the weighing equipment was stored. He used this quite confidently and decided that the pebble was just heavier than the bottle. Ifor completed the sorting with the other objects in the box and then I asked him to check his results. He did this systematically using the balance for many of the comparisons. I then chose three items from the two set rings and asked Ifor to put them in order of weight. He did this quickly and accurately. Then, I chose three items whilst Ifor shut his eyes so that he could not see which set ring they came from. He put these in order, this time without using the balance. Finally, he produced a picture showing the ball and the bottle and he wrote 'the ball is heavier than the bottle.'

Mariam completed the same tasks with me. She worked confidently, made judgements swiftly and competently, using the balance which Ifor had left when she felt it necessary. She recorded her results, using a Venn diagram to show her sorting, with the intersection left empty. Whilst Mariam worked, the classroom assistant came into the room. I asked Mariam to explain to the assistant what she had been doing, which she did accurately and without hesitation, explaining how she made her decisions.

I assessed Ifor as having achieved Ma1/1a because he used sorting, comparing and weighing in this activity. He decided in each case whether to come to a conclusion about the objects from their feel or whether he needed to use a balance which he chose for himself. This indicates attainment of Ma1/2a. He discussed with me, responded to my questions and thus attained Ma1/1b. He asked questions such as, 'What shall I do with this? They both feel the same'. However, he was given little opportunity to describe what he was doing and did not use mathematical terms such as heavier and lighter so he did not achieve Ma1/2b. He achieved Ma1/1c as he was able to use prediction when comparing two objects, but his explanations did not satisfy Ma1/2c as his answers were not responses to the question, 'What would happen if...?'. Ifor attained Ma4/1c because he was able to compare and order several objects before he decided to use the balance. This activity did not give suitable information for Ma5/1a because the sorting was based on criteria which I set, not the child. The evidence which I collected from this activity contributed towards evidence from other contexts about Ifor's attainment in these SoAs.

Mariam was assessed as having achieved Ma1/1a because she had used sorting, comparing and weighing in the activity. She did not select her balance to be used as Ifor had left one available and so was not able to demonstrate Ma1/2a, as Ifor had done. She attained Ma1/1b because she readily talked about her work. She also attained Ma1/2b because of the clear account of her work that she gave to the classroom assistant and because she used appropriate mathematical language such as 'lightest, medium, a bit more than that one, heaviest'. She attained Ma1/1c because she predicted which would be heavier before using a balance. Mariam attained Ma4/1c by comparing the weights of objects without weighing. As with Ifor, the evidence which I collected from this activity contributed towards evidence from other contexts about Mariam's attainment in these SoAs.

This assessment will be taken into account for future planning for both children. Ifor would benefit from being given the opportunity to select his own sorting criteria in order to achieve Ma5/1a. His written record was completed reluctantly and he needs more help and encouragement to record. I did not give him enough opportunity to discuss his work or to ask questions, so that needs to be considered in order that he can attain Ma1/2b. He is probably ready to be assessed for Ma1/2c, so Ifor needs appropriate contexts for 'What would happen if...?' questions.

I should have asked Ifor to put the balance back before I began with Mariam. I feel sure that she could have attained Ma1/2a if given the opportunity to select materials for herself. Mariam lacked confidence when asked the 'What would happen if...?' type of questions and needs opportunities to practise this. As with Ifor, opportunities to select her own criteria will need to be given as Mariam is probably ready to be assessed for Ma5/1a.

The teacher concludes that both children need more opportunity to talk about their mathematics. As Brissenden (1988) states, discussions between children and teacher offer rich opportunities to assess children's understanding of their mathematics. Through the interactions between child and teacher, mathematical vocabulary can be used in its correct context, so that children become confident users of such vocabulary. The teacher in the above example encouraged Ifor through his use of the language 'heavier', 'lighter'. With further encouragement he will soon use such language fluently and in appropriate contexts, as Mariam is already doing.

Activities such as those described above need careful planning. Which aspects of the mathematics curriculum to include, and which SoAs are likely to be assessable need to be considered. However, what has been planned may not be possible in practice. Mariam, for example, did not have the opportunity to choose her own balance. If this had been possible, then further evidence about her attainment could have been obtained. An activity such as the one described above provides information about what children know, understand and are able to do. It also provides information about what the children are working towards, so that teachers can make decisions for forward planning which take into account the children's strengths and growth-point needs.

CASE STUDY

2. Weighing task with Year 2 children

I wanted to assess three Y2 children in my class through an investigational activity. I provided kitchen scales with a dial graduated in grams, a large bucket balance and a rocker balance. There were a number of objects of different weights to be weighed and metric weights and interlocking cubes which could be used as the weights. The metric weights were each too heavy to weigh some of the lighter items. The children were asked to predict which would be the most accurate weighing machine. As only one of the children understood the word 'accurate' I changed this to 'best'. Each child wrote down their own prediction and all chose the kitchen scales. I provided a grid for recording but the children were told that they could choose their own method of recording if they preferred. They all chose to use my grid. They were then asked to weigh the same objects on all three weighing machines.

The teacher's recording grid (see Figures 7.1–7.3) offered no opportunity for the children to record estimation of weight. Improved accuracy in estimation will come with experience of comparison of an estimate with a measure. Children will be assessed on their attainment in estimation in Ma2/3d. However, experience should begin with early measuring activities.

Rosita used a mixture of weights and interlocking cubes to weigh each object. She worked systematically, weighing the same item on each machine in turn before going on to the next object. She did not record 100g and 10g as 110g but as 100g and 10g. She did not always read the kitchen scales accurately. She misread the value of one of the weights that she used. Rosita showed no surprise when she had different results for the same object on different machines.

   Lauren worked slowly. She chose either weights or cubes for each item and she recorded that a light sponge did not work. Her recording was systematic; her writing ability was not to the same standard as Rosita's. She was not surprised when she obtained different results for the same object on the different balances. I asked her which was the best machine and Lauren said that it was the kitchen scales because they had numbers on them.

Neither Rosita nor Lauren appear to have grasped the principle of conservation of weight, as they showed no surprise at the differences in their results for weighing the same object on different machines. This is an important concept, one which Piaget identified as being 'one of the key indicators of a child's intellectual development' (Haylock and Cockburn, 1989). However, it could also be surmised that both Rosita and Lauren had used a variety of weighing machines in many contexts and were aware of the machines' limitations and inaccuracies.

   Guy worked very slowly with long periods of inactivity; his written work took nearly an hour. He used no units to indicate whether he had used gram weights or cubes and many of his numerals were reversed. One of his results showed a lack of understanding of place value when he wrote '1039'. When he had finished I asked him which was the best machine and he chose the bucket balance and said that the pointer 'helped you to see'. He said the rocker balance 'didn't stay still', which was true as this balance took a long time to settle.

It is possible that Guy did use units in his recording. Rather than '1039' this may be '103g' and '39g'. He may have forgotten the meaning of what he had written when his teacher asked him about it.

   I assessed the children's attainment as follows. Rosita attained Ma1/1a as she used the weighing equipment provided for the task. She selected from the provided weights and cubes which indicated that she was working towards Ma1/2a but I needed to see her make her choice from a more open selection before I could be sure that she had attained this. She used both standard and non-standard units. However, she showed no need for consistency and so I could not assess her as having achieved Ma2/2d.

This is a very strict interpretation of Ma2/2d, which asks children to 'Recognise the need for standard units of measurement'. The example refers to children identifying things which are commonly measured in standard units. The children were given both metric

Figure 7.1 Rosita's completion of a record sheet for a weighing activity

Object	Scales	Weight
cork		51
cork		10
cork	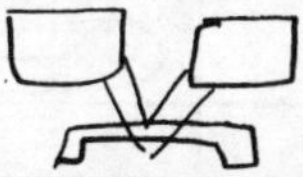	1 cube
orange	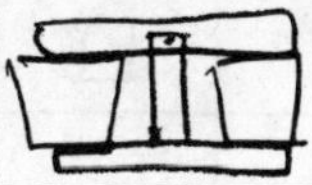	100g & 10g 5 cubes
orange		100g & 3g
orange	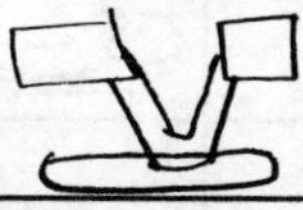	100g 10g 2 cubes
cup		20g & two cubes
cup		25g
cup	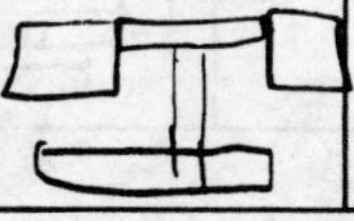	30g

Rosita

Figure 7.2 Lauren recorded all the objects and balances she used and some of the results of the weighings

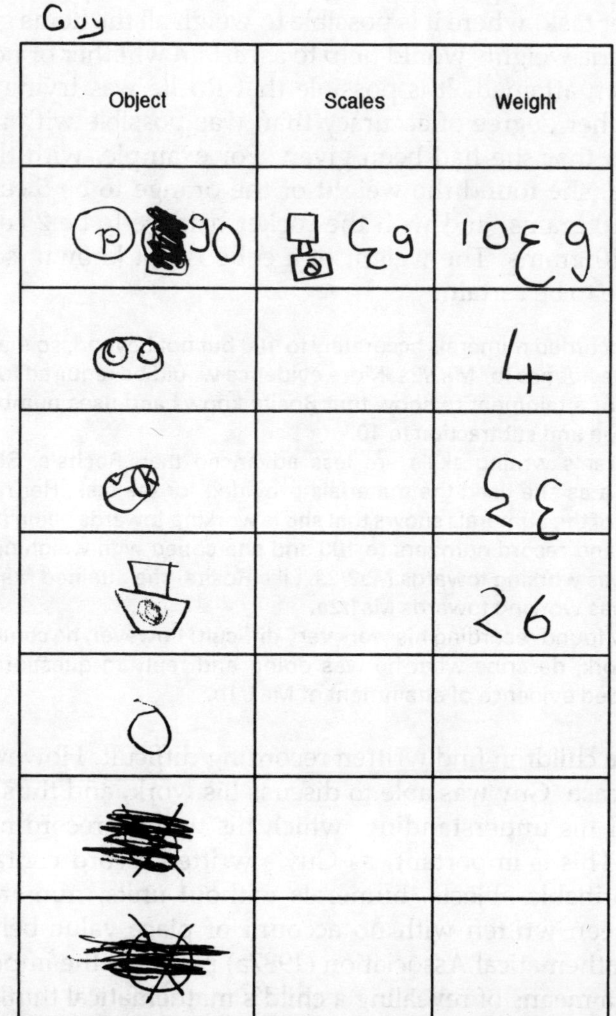

Figure 7.3 Guy took nearly an hour to produce this record of a weighing activity

weights and cubes to use as weights and, as they found, some items were too light to be weighed with any of the metric weights. Another task, where it is possible to weigh all the items given with the metric weights would help to ascertain whether or not Ma2/2d had been attained. It is possible that Rosita was trying to weigh to a higher degree of accuracy than was possible with the metric weights that she had been given. For example, with the bucket balance, she found the weight of the orange to be 5 cubes more than 110 grams, and with the rocker balance to be 2 cubes more than 110 grams. The weight of a cube is not known, so it is not possible to be certain.

She recorded numerals accurately to 100 but not beyond, so that there was some evidence for Ma2/2a. More evidence would be required for this statement of attainment to show that Rosita knows and uses number facts for addition and subtraction to 10.

Lauren's writing skills are less advanced than Rosita's. She attained Ma1/1a as she used the materials provided for the task. Her recording of some of the numerals shows that she is working towards being able to read, write and record numbers to 100 and she coped with weighing in grams. She was working towards Ma2/2a. Like Rosita, she attained Ma1/1a and 1c and was working towards Ma1/2a.

Guy found recording his work very difficult; however, he could talk about his work, describe what he was doing and reply to questions and thus provided evidence of attainment of Ma1/1b.

Some children find written recording difficult. However, in the above case, Guy was able to discuss his work, and thus show the level of his understanding, which his written recording did not show. This is important, as Guy's written record contains some unidentifiable objects, numerals without units, numerals which have been written with no account of place value being taken. The Mathematical Association (1987a) points to the importance of talk as a means of revealing a child's mathematical thinking, both for concepts which have been understood and misunderstandings and why they have occurred.

None of the children was sure of the meaning of the word 'accurate' and they were unconcerned if the different weighing machines gave different 'weights' for the same objects. They would all benefit from activities which encouraged the understanding of conservation of weight. Rosita will be able to show her attainment of Ma2/2a through her number work. Lauren needs more help with recording numerals, both with reversals and the order of the digits; this will help her to move towards attaining Ma2/2a. Guy, particularly, needs help to gain in confidence with his recording skills.

The teacher of Rosita, Lauren and Guy had set herself clear objectives for this assessment activity. However, her anxiety to record National Curriculum levels of achievement overshadowed her observation of the children's work and stopped her from responding to what the children did say and do. Lauren's observation showed that she had observed that the sponge was too light for its weight to be recorded on any of the weighing machines with the weights available. Why had the sponge been included amongst the objects available? What was its purpose? Why did Lauren find that the numerals on the kitchen scales made it the best machine for her?

Did Rosita and Lauren understand the principle of conservation of weight? The teacher's concern was that the children did not understand the word 'accurate'. Was this word part of the classroom vocabulary? The children seemed unconcerned that the different weighing machines gave different results for the same objects. Had this been discussed with the children during previous activities which used these machines, or were the machines so inaccurate that the children's expecatations were that the results would be different?

The danger in using National Curriculum Attainment Targets as the sole focus for assessment is that the teacher can be distracted from a much more important piece of evidence of the children's learning, or their lack of understanding. The pressure to record children's learning achievements within the National Curriculum framework is immense. To devise specific activities in order to identify particular learning can detract from more important observations. It is also costly in time, if each child needs to be assessed in this way for each statement of attainment.

Both of the teachers reported above had made clear interpretations of the meanings of the statements of attainment. It is essential that there is national agreement on the meanings implied within individual SoAs so that there is local and national consistency within the assessment system. Evidence from ENCA I Project (SEAC, 1992) identifies a lack of agreement of the meanings of key words and ideas within the SoAs and points to the need for more agreement trial meetings between local primary schools. This would be useful as it would set standard interpretations for teacher assessment, which would match with SAT interpretations and thus lead to more confidence amongst teachers in their ability to assess children's attainment through agreed criteria.

CASE STUDY

3. Unplanned teacher assessment

Within any classroom there will be unplanned events during the day. These can be a child bringing in an object of interest for others to see, a child producing an unexpectedly good outcome from an activity, or the realization by the teacher that a child has not understood a concept. These events can be useful sources of evidence of attainment. In some schools there is a policy of each teacher making a short note of such unexpected evidence at the end of the day. The following extract comes from Chapter 4. 'Introduction of calculators to a Year 4 class', by Steve Bryant. This describes a conversation between Steve and two children.

The most positive aspect of the implementation of this work was the discussion that was generated. The children wanted to talk about numbers, they wanted to show me what they had found and they wanted to find out more. One particular conversation was about the division of 33 by 3. Two children came to tell me, with confidence, that their calculators were not working. They had entered what they thought was correct, but were presented with a line of numbers.

Teacher:	It's 3 divided by 33 is that what you're putting in?
Karen:	11 this time it turned up.
Teacher:	Is that the right answer?
Karen:	Yes. But the calculators are wrong!
Teacher:	Wait a minute. What did you say? Divide 3 by 33? Is that right?
Laura:	You can't divide it.
Teacher:	Why?
Laura:	Because you've got 3 which is less than 33.

The conversation continued with a discussion of whether 3 divided by 33 is the same as 33 divided by 3. The children had been surprised at the result that they had obtained as there had been a recurring number ($3/33 = 0.09090909$). They soon realized that the two inputs, ie, 3/33 and 33/3, were quite different. This was the first time that most children had dealt with a decimal fraction of a whole number.

This extract provides evidence of the children's thinking. They are working towards Ma2/4a and d. They realized that the order in which information is entered into the calculator does matter. There is also the beginning of the realization that a small number can be divided by a larger one and that, using a calculator, this will produce a decimal fraction. Karen considered the calculator result to be unreasonable based upon what she had expected as a result;

that is, she expected 33 divided by 3 to give 11. Karen had not developed a strategy for dealing with a decimal fraction, (3 divided by 33) other than to state that a small number could not be divided by a larger one. However, with their teacher's help, both children had now begun to investigate decimal fractions, how they can occur and ways of producing them. They are working towards Ma1/4b as they demonstrated an awareness of the need to interpret the problem into appropriate calculator language. Neither Karen nor Laura have demonstrated that they have as yet attained these SoAs, but are working at this level. For Steve there are clear implications for forward planning. Both children would benefit from activities which encourage them to use their calculators for division. Estimating the size of an answer and then checking that with their result would be useful experience of prediction. However, what of the other children in Steve's class? This was the first time that most of them had encountered decimal fractions. What was appropriate for Karen and Laura would also probably be an appropriate next stage for others in the class.

Sometimes an overheard conversation between two children can be a most revealing source of children's level of understanding. The following extract comes from Chapter 3. 'The use of a programmable toy in the reception class', by Wendy Proctor.

Wendy introduced the children to using combinations of commands for PIP. The children found that PIP could be made to turn and to move forward or back, using just one series of commands. She noted the conversation between two children:

Adam:	Let's make him [PIP] go over there to the cupboard.
Barry:	I'll make him go. [He pressed Forward 3 (30cm) then Right 9. GO.]
Barry:	Oh no, he's gone the wrong way.
Adam:	I'll have him back now. [He pressed Back 2, Right 9, GO.] [PIP travelled much further than was expected.]
Barry:	Did you make him do all that?
Adam:	No. I forgot to Clear Memory. Silly me. Let me do it again.

Both Adam and Barry demonstrated that they had formed a prediction for PIP's expected movement. With evidence from other contexts this would lead to an attainment of Ma1/1c. Adam, though, was also able to identify the 'bug' in his programming and to explain to Barry what was wrong. With evidence from other contexts he would attain Ma1/1b and be working towards Ma1/2b.

On some occasions when such a conversation is overheard, it can be even more revealing if the teacher joins in and asks further questions. In this case, perhaps Adam and Barry could be encouraged to predict how many PIP units forward are needed, to talk about how accurate their prediction was, using mathematical language such as nearer, further, longer, shorter. Asking a question such as, 'What would happen if you asked PIP to go forward five from the cupboard' would encourage prediction.

Assessment of children's learning has always been part of the teacher's role. It is important that assessment is of good quality and that it identifies what children have attained as well as pointing to the next stage of development. The following six points can help to make assessment of mathematics part of the teaching style adopted and thus integral to the children's learning.

i. *Autonomy*. Children who can act independently in the classroom, who can take some responsibility for their own learning, will allow their teacher more quality time to work with individuals or with small groups. Adam and Barry were able to work independently from their teacher; she had set them a task which they understood. They collaborated with each other in order to carry out the task, acting as independent learners, using a mistake in input to PIP as a useful learning tool, and without needing to ask for their teacher's help.

Children who take responsibility for themselves can use extension and reinforcement materials with little teacher intervention, if they finish the set task early. Again, this reduces teacher stress and leaves more time for work with particular children.

ii. *Availability of apparatus*. Classroom arrangement of materials can help children to become more independent. The storage of mathematics materials on accessible, clearly labelled shelves, so that children can access materials when required, will help children to find what they need, when they need it. If they are encouraged to put materials away after use, this system needs little organization by the teacher. However, it is important that children have had time to explore new materials, to find out what they can do with them and know how to use them correctly. Within the heading of apparatus will also come the availability of calculators and IT. Observations by the teacher about the appropriateness of the particular material chosen by a child can indicate a child's understanding of a concept, or acquisition of a particular skill. Ifor, in the first example, chose an appropriate balance for the weighing task. Previous experience of using such apparatus had enabled him to make such a choice.

iii. *Grouping of children.* The teachers who have contributed to this book have, in the main, described activities which have been designed for individuals, pairs or small groups. Some of them introduced a new topic as a whole-class lesson. The purpose of the grouping is very important in mathematics. HMI (1991) points to the over-use of one style of working in the classroom. The report identifies the need for more flexibility in grouping in order to ensure that the organization of the children matches the task to be undertaken. If there is a good match between task and grouping then the children should be able to work without constant teacher intervention.

If the children can work in a variety of groupings, then the teacher can choose the appropriate one for the task. This will ensure that time can be allocated for assessment purposes and that there will be minimum interruptions from other children. ENCA (SEAC, 1992) reports that most teachers in the survey found that assessing children in groups of four or five was the most usual form of organization.

iv. *Use of 'Do Talk Record'.* This is the framework used in the Open University course, 'Developing Mathematical Thinking' (EM 235). The Scottish National Curriculum (SOED, 1991) has adapted this idea; it describes children starting a task, doing the task and reporting on the outcomes in a variety of ways and for a range of audiences and purposes. At any stage in this process children should be encouraged to evaluate what they have achieved. This process is of particular help with planning, teaching and assessing in Ma1, where children should be encouraged to use their mathematical knowledge, skills and understanding in practical situations.

For the teacher this process offers opportunities for assessment at any of the stages. The planning of an investigation and decisions about which materials would be useful, can be useful indicators of the children's understanding of the task, its purpose and of the range of strategies which would be useful to employ in its resolution. Whilst children are actively engaged on the task, there may be opportunities for the teacher to ask questions, to observe the chosen strategies in operation and how the children use them, and to listen to discussion between the children engaged in the task. Recording of the process used and rough working which children may adopt, can provide evidence of attainment in itself and does not need to be re-written neatly in order to provide that evidence. The end result can include a written report, evidence of data collection, graphical representation of the data collected, or a range of solutions to the problem set. Any of these can offer evidence of attainment. A spoken report, in which children discuss their findings, the processes which they used and the appropriateness of their results, can, again, provide evidence of attainment.

v. *Personal qualities*. In order to be effective, learners of mathematics need to develop positive attitudes. The personal qualities to be developed have been identified within the Non-Statutory Guidance for Mathematics (NCC, 1991, paragraph 5.13) as motivation, flexible and creative thinking, perseverance, taking control of one's own work, independence of thought and action, cooperation within a group and systematic work habits. It is through the development of these qualities, vital for success in mathematics learning, that children's attitudes towards mathematics will be established. The Non-Statutory Guidance further suggests that teachers should encourage: fascination with mathematics, interest and motivation, pleasure and enjoyment from mathematical activity, appreciation of the power, purpose and relevance of mathematics, satisfaction derived from a sense of achievement and confidence in an ability to do mathematics at an appropriate level.

Another useful teaching and learning strategy is described as 'Plan Do Review', a programme for pre-school groups (Hohmann *et al.*, 1979). Children are encouraged to make a plan before they begin work and to report back on the effectiveness of their plan and of the work which they have undertaken. This report can provide evidence of children's ability to form a coherent work plan, to concentrate in order to carry it out, and their awareness of the appropriateness of what has been done. If used in conjunction with 'Do Talk Record', there will be evidence of children's mathematical achievements and of the development of personal qualities or attitudes towards mathematics.

Children's personal qualities and their attitudes towards mathematics can directly affect their achievement. The development of qualities such as motivation, perseverance, independence of thought and action and the ability to cooperate and collaborate within a group, and of attitudes such as interest, satisfaction and confidence, will help children to have positive images of themselves and thus to be more effective learners. As Lloyd-Jones and Bray (1986) report, children need to have these areas assessed as well as curriculum content levels, as these positive attitudes and personal qualities are regarded as necessary life skills.

vi. *Interpretation of the meaning of Statements of Attainment*. Some of these are open to a range of interpretations. Within a school there needs to be agreement as to what constitutes evidence for any statement of attainment, and for this there needs to be agreement on the meaning of the SoA. As will be seen in the next section, there is a need for agreement across schools and, it will be argued, for national agreement.

Record-keeping

ENCA (SEAC, 1992) reports little evidence of useful records being passed from one teacher to the next. Within a subject such as mathematics, which contains such a wide range of knowledge, skills and understanding, records need to be clear, in a format which is easily accessible to others, and to contain evidence which is useful for forward planning. In this section the record-keeping practice in mathematics in three schools will be considered first, followed by a discussion of transfer records for children passing from one school to another.

CASE STUDY

4. Record-keeping at two schools from the same LEA

The following two case studies come from the mathematics coordinators of two schools in the same borough. Both schools had recently changed the published schemes which they used, the first school to a scheme which had been on the market for some years, the second to a new publication. The mathematics coordinator of the first school said:

Record keeping began with the introduction of the new scheme which we adopted. The first attempt consisted of a sheet which included the areas of the scheme covered, the strategies and processes with which the child was familiar and any supplementary work covered. There was a copy of this sheet for each child's record. The records did not include any comments about the quality of the child's work, nor of what the child knew, understood and could do. The use of this form of record sheet was called into question by the staff. As the children worked in ability groups for mathematics, it was agreed to keep group records of what had been covered. Each teacher devised their own record for children's attainment; this was wasteful as it meant that the format of the records which contained the attainment levels for each child were individually devised by each teacher. There was no uniformity and no agreement on what should be recorded nor on what comprised evidence.

The records which each teacher kept may have been useful to that individual, but with no staff agreement upon how such records needed to be kept, the evidence obtained would not assist subsequent teachers in planning appropriate work. Records of what has been covered are not the same as records of children's learning achievements. The former describes merely what has been attempted; the latter describes what has been learned. There is a need for both, in order to build a profile of experience and achievement for each child. The teachers in this school do not appear to have given much thought to the purpose for which records need to be kept. As there was no agreement on record-keeping it is reasonable to assume that the teachers had not examined their assessment practice, as Winteridge (1989) recommends, nor had they included record-keeping and assessment within the policy statement for teaching mathematics.

HMI (1992) finds that the most useful records contain the data for each child for each AT and written comments, perhaps describing the task completed which had provided the evidence of attainment. The LEA had produced a record sheet on which such evidence could be recorded; however, most teachers found it very time-consuming to complete and thus it was not in general use in this school, although it was being used at the second school. The mathematics coordinator of the second school reported:

One of the advantages of the mathematics scheme which we use is that it has its own record-keeping system which is linked to the National Curriculum. The LEA has produced record cards, on which we record when children have achieved a statement of attainment, what evidence of achievement has been retained or a statement of teacher observation. However, for mathematics this is time-consuming and the staff feel the need to streamline the system and to cut down the amount of record-keeping. What is necessary is for there to be shared understandings between schools of the interpretation of the meaning of statements of attainment. This has happened between primary schools and at the primary/secondary interface. The records of attainment which the staff keep are available to parents, but these need further explanation as they're not easy to understand.

HMI (1992) finds that, as in this school, many teachers are keeping samples of children's work to support judgements about attainment. HMI suggests that the most useful work to keep is that which has been annotated to show which SoAs have been attained. HMI (1991) advises that the tasks set should also be described on work which is kept as evidence. For mathematics, evidence of attainment can be found in children's rough workings; if this is so, then this should be kept – there is no need for a child to re-write this. However, a best copy of other work should be kept in order to show evidence of recording in its final form.

CASE STUDY

5. Gathering evidence of attainment

What both of the above schools found difficult was identifying a form of record-keeping which was manageable and also useful. In the following example, from a village school in the west country, the teachers have found a method which they find practical, although it is still time-consuming. The teaching head had introduced the Centre for Language in Primary Education (1990) record system. She had worked on the development team in ILEA prior to her move to her present school. She kept a diary of observations for each child and used the sample sheet headings to keep detailed records of observations which she believed were significant. The record was kept for English and science in the same way, so that conferences with children and parents could be held for all three subject areas. The head describes the process.

I keep a record, such as the following, of anything which appears significant to the children's stage of development.
    Alex and James, both Year 5, worked together on a broken keys calculator activity. I wrote the following in my record book, using the CLPE sample sheets, for Alex and James.

Context and background information about activity:
    Exploring calculator – calculator has broken keys. Given as challenge to children by me. Working collaboratively with James. Sustained activity.

General impression of the child's approach:
    Alex – Initially reluctant to try on his own but more confident when began

to work with James. Became more confident when he realized there was more than one answer.

James – Started off by saying, 'This is easy, I know how to do it'. Very confident and involved in activity. Straight in to activity.

Strategies and mathematical processes the child used:
Alex – Initially copied James' ideas. Tending to sit, watch and listen. Talked to me about what he'd done. Could explain what they'd done but not always why. Explained he'd had an idea which had got James started.

James – Seemed to have idea in mind and started straight away. When couldn't work part out suggested it couldn't be done. Didn't discuss much with Alex. Made and tested predictions. Talked enthusiastically about it.

Child's own response to the activity:
Alex – Initially not interested. Became more involved, but never completely absorbed. Didn't seem able to use calculator always.

James – Very interested and enjoyed it. Used one of the calculators to help him check he'd done it.

Knowledge and understanding shown by the child:
Alex – Knows that numbers can be broken down to make equivalent numbers. Some understanding of use of brackets.

James – Understanding of approaches which might provide solution. Able to think around problem.

What this sample shows about the child's mathematical development:
Alex – Lacks confidence, particularly in problem-solving situation. Is more confident when working with a confident person.

James – Shows his confidence and interest. Highlights difficulties in working collaboratively, tends to work alongside rather than with. Lacks perseverance if answer not immediately obvious.

Experience/support needed to further development
Alex – Opportunities to become a leader in a problem-solving situation. More extended problem-solving. More calculator work.

James – Needs opportunities to work collaboratively and on extended challenge.

This record forms the basis for future planning for both children. It identifies strengths and growth points, in both mathematical attainment and in personal qualities and attitudes. From this observation the teacher would plan suitable activities for each of the two children. The LEA also provides a record card which covers all ATs and SoAs for the core curriculum. This is completed from the evidence sheets which the teachers keep during the year.

The following is from the infant teacher, at the same school. The children had worked, either in pairs, or independently of each other, on the same activity but at their own level. The activity was called 'Counting and guessing'. Both children reported here were Year 2.

Context and background information about the activity:

Nigel – Practical activity. I saw a need to extend his knowledge of numbers beyond 250. Worked alone, but compared groups made with others.

Martin – Practical activity. I wanted to check his ability to count and use numbers beyond 100. Working in a pair over a short period of time.

Overall impression of the child's approach:

Nigel – Independent. Very involved. Decided to count in tens then in ones. Lost count (blamed somebody else) but continued to count in ones.

Martin – Independent. Read activity sheet then chose patterns. Realized he needed to make a chart, used one of my examples and faithfully reproduced it.

Strategies and mathematical processes the child used:

Nigel – Guess of paper clips was extraordinarily accurate: 199 out of 200. Knew one less than 50 was 49. Even though everyone else was beginning to count in tens, Nigel continued to count in ones. Interpreted results accurately. Paper clips are small so get more in your hands. Discussed results with Jes. Made and tested predictions.

Martin – Chose buttons; counted individually and then decided he could count in twos or tens. Decided to check results. Placed in groups of tens. Chose materials himself. Decided to get the biggest handful of paperclips but soon lost interest in counting them. Not accurate with his recording on the chart. Quite messy. Numbers didn't tally. Realized he had much more than his original guess. Needed help counting.

Child's own response to the activity;

Nigel – Really enjoyed the activity. Found it a challenge. Was confident in his ability to use numbers to 200.

Martin – Found it interesting. Said he found it easy. With probing he admitted to finding the counting hard.

Knowledge and understanding shown by the child;

Nigel – Was able to write numbers to 20. Made accurate predictions. Is able to count in tens. Could count orally numbers to 100.

Martin – Could count in tens up to 90 but forgot what came afterwards until prompted. Could write numbers to 200 but needed help counting to 295. Guesses were about half what they should have been.

What this sample shows about the child's mathematical development:

Nigel – Confident in using numbers to 200. Needs to think more about sorting in groups. Should have used tens to group his paper clips.

Martin – Martin is working at Level 2. Needs more reinforcement in this area. Individual investigations: initially working with groups to compare results.

Experience/support needed to further development:

Nigel – More extended work needed, perhaps using pegboards to see if he can deduce that pegs are in rows of ten and therefore an aid to counting. AT1/2abc; AT2/2ab.

Martin – Help is needed in setting out work neatly and accurately. AT1/1abc;AT2/2a.

Here, the teacher has added attainment target references for those SoAs which she felt were being worked towards. This process would be repeated in a different context later in the term, so that for each child there would be a number of in-depth observation records available as evidence of attainment. The following comes from the same teacher's record book. This is the record for Ellen, a Year 1 child, who worked at an activity for number bonds to 10.

Context and background information about the activity:
Exploring number pairs. Testing number bonds to 10. Worked alone. Short activity.

Overall impression of the child's approach:
Independent. Was able to decide what equipment was needed. Worked out bonds practically first, then put onto paper.

Strategies and mathematical processes the child used:
Used knowledge of number and counting to correctly put down the number pairs. Recording was rather untidy. Confusing addition sign and multiplication sign.

Child's own response to the activity:
Sustained interest over period of session.

Knowledge and understanding shown by the child:
Understood the number bonds to 10.

What this sample shows about the child's mathematical development. Experience/support needed to further development:
Can move on to explore further number patterns.

This indicated forward planning needs for Ellen, rather than listing her National Curriculum attainments. The following observations were made about Jerry, in Year 1. The second observation was made six weeks after the first, during the spring term.

1. Measuring chart, measuring using a tape measure and recording lengths from waist to knee, length of waist to ankle, from shoulder to waist and the length of the arm.
   Jerry coped extremely well, reading the directions and recording accurately in the box. 'You're taller than me, you have a shorter arm'. He did have to ask Carrie which way the numbers went round. (Being left-handed he finds this difficult.)
   Jerry understands the language of measurement and was able to apply this correctly, eg, taller, shorter, smaller, bigger, as big as, etc.

2. Formal session to test knowledge of number bonds to 10. Worked independently using apparatus to help him. Understood the number bonds and was beginning to see a pattern emerging.

Both teachers found the format of the CLPE record a useful means of recording children's attainment. They commented that it was time-consuming, but that it enabled them to build up a reasonably complete picture of each child, that it gave useful evidence not just of what had been attained, but also of needs for forward planning. Gipps (1990) reports that teachers who use teacher assessment as a tool to identify children's next stage of learning are able to match tasks more accurately to children's needs; this is confirmed by these teachers' observations of their children's learning.

Both teachers had involved the children in assessment of their progress. The child's own response to the activity has been recorded in some cases; this can help to improve children's self-confidence and self-esteem and can also help children to accept that there will be areas of mathematics where they need to increase their knowledge and understanding. Self-assessment by children of their mathematical achievements can form part of a record of achievement, which normally focuses upon success rather than failure, as Connor (1991) identifies, although recent developments have asked children to consider areas where they will need to concentrate. Examples of such records, where children comment on successes and on areas which they found more difficult can be found in Stocker (1990).

Neither of these teachers feels constrained by the National Curriculum in their assessments of children's achievements. They show that they have considered the programmes of study and what these imply for children's learning, as well as the development of children's personal qualities and attitudes towards mathematics. From their assessment they identify which parts of the National Curriculum have been achieved, rather than identifying SoAs and assessing for knowledge and understanding of these. This allows the teachers to identify next steps in learning.

6. Transfer records

These are records of mathematical attainment which are passed from one school to another, usually on cross-phase transfer. T following account comes from the head of department for m matics of the town high school, which accepts all abilities ' the local primary schools, both town and rural.

CASE STUDY

When children transfer to us at 11, it is interesting to see that although some of the primary schools are so small that they only send us, say, five children, these five are likely to represent the range of abilities at 11. Most of the children who come to us are used to working on an individualized programme of work. Also, the children who have been taught in vertically grouped classes tend to be much better at topic work, where there is a group approach. This is a common approach, through a topic, in order to cater for the wide range of abilities in vertically grouped classes. Children from the small primary schools are much more adaptable to topic and group work than those who come from a single year class where the work has been particularly structured towards their age and ability.

We do not get detailed records from the primary school before the children start with us. Records will arrive in my department after the children have started in September, so we teach the children in mixed ability groups until the autumn half-term. What we receive is the LEA record card with the list of attainment targets and a level for each. Some schools have filled in these records in great detail, marking each time a topic has been visited and when it has been understood; others have just ticked a box – we need to find out what these marks mean. There has been no standardization, although the headteachers of all the schools decided that these records would be used. Something that we haven't done yet and want to do is to consider the statements of attainment and to agree across the pyramid on our interpretation of them; this would help to sort out this muddle.

The scheme which we use is an individualized one so that we can slot pupils in at an appropriate point for them. Once we receive the records from the feeder primary schools we set the pupils, based upon these records and our own observations of the pupils. We check to see which topics the pupils have covered and understood, as it is a waste of their time repeating work which they already understand. We identify which topics they need to concentrate on and at which level. You must remember that we are dealing with an ability spread of Level 1 to Level 7 for our 11-year-olds. We hope that all of this now avoids that dreadful scenario where the primary school thinks that the secondary school has ignored all their hard work with the pupils. We've had a lot of really positive feedback about our present system of receiving the new intake. We're also using the organization methods which the pupils are used to, that is, mainly individualized work, with some group topic or investigational work. The pupils have been very positive about this. We also have visits from the pupils before they start with us. These begin in Year 5, so that the school and we are familiar by the time that they start at 11.

The term 'topic' is used in the above to indicate a mathematical topic, such as pattern, rather than a cross-curricular theme or topic. HMI (1991) finds that cross-phase records were often of little use in helping teachers to make reasonable decisions about curricular progress for individual children; similar findings can be found in

Cockcroft (1982). Again, the need for agreement about the meaning of statements of attainment has been raised – there is a need for
country-wide agreement. Perhaps documents such as the recently
published INSET Resources (NCC, 1992) will help to clarify matters. The above also indicates a need for schools to have an agreement on how they will fill in the records, so that the receiving
school receives evidence which has a common basis.

There is also a need for there to be agreement upon what is implied within the programmes of study and their associated range of
experiences. The statements of attainment can cover a wide-rang-
ing section of the programme of study. Evidence of attainment will
need to come from a variety of contexts within the programme of
study, not just from the outcome of one activity.

Conclusion

This chapter has considered the purposes of assessment in mathematics. Assessment of children's knowledge, skills and understanding against the Statements of Attainment for Mathematics
must be completed, by law. It has been argued that children's
personal qualities and attitudes towards mathematics should also
be assessed in order that children can be encouraged to develop
positive attitudes which will lead them to successful mathematical
learning.

Each school described here has developed its own form of
record-keeping which then transfers to the LEA form. What is
recorded needs to contain evidence of attainment both for SoAs
and for personal qualities and attitudes. The purpose of such
records is two fold: on the one hand, they provide evidence of
attainment by children which contributes towards formal assessment procedures; on the other, these records provide the basic
evidence upon which forward planning can be based.

A clear need has been expressed, both by contributors to this
chapter and by HMI, for agreement to be reached on the meaning
of SoAs. Recent publications from NCC (1992) suggest that an attempt is being made at national level to clarify meanings. However, teachers need opportunities to meet and discuss individual
SoAs, to compare evidence and to come to an agreement as to their
meaning.

Chapter 8

Looking Forward

So much has been achieved by teachers and children in such a short time span: in three years, teachers have implemented the National Curriculum Orders for Mathematics, devised record-keeping procedures and, at Key Stage 1, undertaken SATs administration. In this chapter, these achievements will be considered in detail. Interview evidence, from parents, student teachers and a chairperson of governors, is used to highlight achievements and those factors which need further consideration. The chapter is in four sections:

- Current developments in primary mathematics teaching.
- Community attitudes towards primary school mathematics teaching.
- Teacher confidence in the mathematics curriculum.
- Ways forward.

Current developments in primary mathematics teaching

Primary schools' review of their practice in mathematics teaching led to revision of school policy statements. In Chapter 6 it was seen that this review could lead to identification of content missing from a schools' mathematics syllabus, and remedial action being taken in order to provide suitable teaching and learning materials as support. The review of policy statements also took into account the teaching styles which were used, how effective these were and in which situations, and, as a result, teachers identified the need for change. In some schools, this review led to the search for a replacement published scheme, which would support teachers and children. Some publishers have already produced their National Curriculum Mathematics scheme; others have new schemes in the pipeline. Publishers are aware that this is a big business opportunity and that a review of current practice will, inevitably, show up shortcomings in the school's current scheme. Schools which adopt a particular scheme will become a captive market for at least five years, until the school carries out its next major review, as there are on-going costs for replacement consumable materials. For schools which used a scheme which was seriously out of step with the National Curriculum, the change to teaching materials which took account of the Statutory Orders was a positive step forward. However, in schools where change seems to have been made without whole staff approval, this has led to disaffected teachers who did not have sufficient support to bring about the changes which were asked of them.

The case studies reported in this book show that more emphasis is now placed upon children taking responsibility for their own learning. Children are encouraged to be more autonomous, to find materials for themselves and to put them away again. Children are encouraged to work collaboratively and to discuss their work with each other and their teacher. There is evidence of children being encouraged to become more independent: in Chapter 2, the case study of 'A school environment trail devised by a group of Year 4 and 5 slow learners' showed how children with little confidence in their ability as mathematicians could be encouraged to use and extend their knowledge and understanding in problem-solving situations in order to devise their own maths trail, and then to undertake a leadership role with other children who used the trail.

The existence of Attainment Target Ma1, Using and Applying Mathematics, has contributed towards the encouragement of more positive attitudes to mathematics. Teachers' response to Ma1 has led to more practical mathematics, the use of problem-solving and enquiry. In Chapter 3, the case studies describing the introduction of Logo showed that the 'using and applying' approach led children to begin to form predictions, to use trial and improvement strategies, to ask and answer questions, and to discuss their work with each other.

Some teachers have developed particular aspects of the mathematics curriculum in order to introduce a new topic to the whole school. Children using calculators for enquiry and problem-solving activities are described in Chapter 4. The teachers involved were surprised by how readily their children began to use large numbers and they became aware of what a powerful tool the calculator could be and of the need for a whole-school policy to be developed and implemented. Similarly, the teachers who developed maths trails and Logo activities found that the children developed mathematical skills and that they became more confident as mathematicians. The Logo projects show a similar result to the calculator projects, as children used large numbers, outside the traditional curriculum.

Teachers who have contributed to this book have shown that their children are developing methods of mental, and pencil and paper calculation. In some instances this has been through the use of calculators or Logo; in other cases this has been achieved through children investigating pattern in number, using problem-solving and enquiry stategies and skills. For others, this has been achieved through maths trails, where children have been set, or have set themselves, a problem which has needed a resolution.

The debate about topic work and its educational desirability has intensified since the publication of Alexander *et al.*'s discussion paper (1992). However, the experiences of the teachers who contributed to Chapter 5, which considered planning for mathematics learning, suggest that it is the quality of the initial planning, the decisions about what the children's needs are, and the vehicle for this learning, or the contexts, which are of fundamental importance, rather than whether or not the learning will take place through subject teaching or through themes or topics. For some teachers who used a cross-curricular topic approach which involved mathematics in other areas of the curriculum, the children's experience was a very rich one. Val Pendleton's children, in 'Identification of specific mathematics teaching points to be developed through a cross-curricular topic of pattern', produced writing in which they explained what numbers were. They showed their understanding of ordinal, cardinal and nominal number in the plays they wrote in the English strand of their topic. Within the same project, collaboration between mathematics and music was strengthened so that identification of pattern in music is now linked to algebraic pattern.

None of the teachers who contributed to this book made any comment about differences in performance between girls and boys. Recent evidence from the APU finds that there is far less difference in performance between girls and boys in mathematics at age 14 than used to be the case. It can be speculated that this has depended upon equality of entitlement throughout these children's mathematical education. The enhanced performance of boys compared with girls, noted in the Cockcroft Report (1982), has been recognized by their teachers and, as a result, it seems that girls have been encouraged in those areas in which in the past they have performed less well than boys.

Community attitudes towards primary school mathematics teaching

Parental attitudes towards mathematics teaching may not coincide with those of teachers nor with the National Curriculum requirements. Ann and Paul Lewis have five children, all boys, aged 13, 11, twins aged 7 and a baby of four months. They are not 'typical' parents, perhaps, as they are active in local politics and they understand how to make the education system work for them. The twins attend the school which their parents chose, rather than the one designated for the part of the town in which they live. The older boys attended a nursery school then a first school in another county until the family moved to its present home. The conversations with Ann and Paul in this section were collected by taped interview during one morning in November 1992. Both Ann and Paul are reasonably confident in their own mathematical ability, as the following extract shows.

CASE STUDY

Interviewer: You feel quite confident about maths.

Ann: He's got O-level which is more than I've got. There are some areas where I'm not confident. I can add up and take away. I worked in a bank for 11 years and had to learn to do exchange rates for foreign currency without a calculator by long division. I suppose I understand a lot of things in maths. I did CSE maths. I wonder if some of the maths children do would actually equip children for later life. It's important that they understand the money that they've got in their pockets so that when they go to a shop they're not short-changed. They need to know how to handle their money. How to budget correctly. Now a lot of the problems that come up in later life, when people go out to work and they have plenty of money in their pockets, and they don't allow for the fact that they're given a set amount each week and they've got to manage their money. It's all very well and good having all these various maths things in the National Curriculum but are children really being taught basic life skills? I think probably they're not.

Interviewer: When would you want them to start learning this?

Ann: Well, they see on the TV all these advertisements for toys. Only £16, only £20. They have no idea of the value. If they have £10 for their birthday, then they will say that they have lots of money. But they have no idea what it is worth in relation to things in the shops. We feel we have to shield the twins from wasting their money. The twins don't seem to be able to work out simple problems, like how many 25p chocolate bars you can get for 50p. They need to be able to do this sort of thing.

Paul: Back in my father's time the skilled machinists had to make their own tools. They learnt how to do this as apprentices and the tools had to be so accurate that they could work with them later on. But the apprenticeships have gone. You were signed up for life. I was asked when I was 12 if I wanted to be apprenticed to my father's firm.

Ann and Paul saw the ability to use mathematics as a life skill. Paul had just been made redundant at the time of this interview and preparation for the world of work was very important to him. Both parents wanted their children to be successful at school and to acquire the skills which would enable them to be successful in adulthood. The conversation continued with a discussion about what Ann and Paul, as parents, expected their 7-year-old twins to learn in mathematics.

Ann: At first school, up to 9, I've noticed a difference between what the older boys were taught and the younger boys. I presume it's down to the National Curriculum. I expect my boys to learn how to add, subtract, multiply and divide, to understand about money. I've noticed that the younger boys have not had much teaching about money at school. It seems to be ignored. We used to live in another county and it was different there. The boys were encouraged to join the school bank. They had a play shop in the classroom which they were encouraged to use with money. But they also had this at playgroup, and when they went to nursery. The younger boys didn't go to nursery. I've noticed a vast difference in the education development of the twins compared to their older brothers.

Interviewer: Why do you think that is?

Ann: I put some of this down to nursery experience. The older boys had a year of learning things at nursery before they went to school. The twins didn't have that and they didn't start school until they were rising 5. My second son has had an extra year at school than any of his peers. This has led him to feel frustrated because a lot of things the other children were doing he had already done and he had to do them again.

Alexander *et al.* (1992) point to the need for children's attainments to be monitored so that positive attempts are made to match learning tasks to the needs and abilities of individual children; they suggest that this is aspirational rather than always achievable. However, for Ann and Paul's son, there must have been considerable frustration at repeating work in which he was already competent.

Interviewer: What else is different?

Ann: The younger ones seem to do more and more book work. They just get on with it. I'm not altogether happy with the way the twins are being taught mathematics. There doesn't seem to be the supervision. They're just given the book and they work at it. They're in a class of 34 children and that class had 36 children until recently. In their first term at school they got on really well. Then there was another intake after Christmas and everything which they had done they repeated with the new children. And then after Easter another intake came in and the same thing happened. Then they were given these maths workbooks to do. They never seemed to do work with their teacher. The children have a race to see who can finish the book first. One of the twins is second in the class for maths. Another child is slightly ahead of him. All I can gather is that all they do in maths is work through these books. I don't even know if she teaches them anything.

Discussions with some PGCE primary students identified similar concerns. The students discussed the approach to teaching mathematics in the classrooms where they were based in school.

Sarah: Well, they have a commercial scheme which the children don't seem to enjoy. Cards, books and maths books. The teacher might put some sums on the board and the children just copy them.

Judy: They work with a published maths scheme. They have maths books, workcards and workbooks. That seems to be about the only maths they seem to do.

Liz: We use workbooks. I find it hard to follow what it is the children are supposed to be doing. It involves so much colouring in.

Peter: I haven't seen any teaching of concepts going on. I'm in Year 2 and all the children seem to do is basic addition. It's workcard- and workbook-based so if the children don't understand then they just go back and do an earlier workcard, so a child will say, 'Oh, I've done this one before'. Then the children have to do each sum in a variety of ways, with brackets, and then with the plus and equals signs. They get really confused.

Only one of the students interviewed commented favourably on the way in which commercial schemes for mathematics were used in her school.

Emma: We use a maths scheme. I think the scheme is rubbish but the teacher's handbook is really good. What our teacher does is to take the activities from the handbook and the children have a really good time. They do practical activities, like using interlocking cubes for an investigation. They really enjoy it. And then she uses the workbook as a check, to finish off a topic. It's what they do when they've done all the practical work. The workbooks are used to show that the children have done something and how well they have understood.

Desforges and Cockburn (1987) identified the race that can develop with workbooks. Children soon become aware of how the scheme operates, which book is 'bottom' and what the order of progression is – what matters is the page of ticks, the race to get to the next book. Understanding of mathematics, enjoyment of mathematics as an aesthetic subject, practical mathematics experiences, problem-solving and enquiry, any of these undertaken away from the workbook scenario can be regarded by the children as not doing proper maths. For teachers who are insecure about teaching mathematics, a published mathematics scheme can provide a carefully regulated 'diet' of mathematics; however, the use of the scheme needs control. Decisions by the teacher about which maths topics the scheme covers well, and which are better covered in a different way, need to be taken. Children need to be engaged with the practical activities which all modern schemes include. either through the teacher's handbook or through pupil books. Handbooks offer advice to teachers on identifying opportunities to teach new concepts so that children can explore the new concept using materials, discuss with their teacher and their peers, make and test predictions, and make generalizations from their learning. Just working through workbooks or workcards provides children with little opportunity to use their mathematics in problem-solving situations and, at worst, can lead to children working through many examples without understanding what is being asked of them. It can also lead to the teacher being busy marking work and there being no time for teaching. Ann and Paul thought that their twin boys were taught in this way.

Interviewer: Do they do practical maths or is it just writing answers in their workbooks?

Ann: I think it's just writing, I don't think they do anything practical.

Paul: They have in the past.

Ann: There's a lot of concentration on practical things in science.

Interviewer: So, do the twins mainly do number?

Ann and Paul: Yes!

Ann: And they've done some bar graphs.

Interviewer: Do they use calculators?

Paul: No.

Ann: The older boys do.

Paul: The twins used the computer last year, but not this year. They have used a programmable toy (Big Trak) and then a floor turtle.

Interviewer: Do they learn their tables?

Both parents laughed.

Ann: Not that I'm aware of. We had great difficulty with the older boys because they didn't learn their tables at first school. When they got to middle school they were in trouble because they didn't know their tables. I told Thomas the only way to learn tables was to learn them parrot fashion, the way we had learnt them. He didn't like that. We went to his teacher. She said that unless he learns his tables he's going to be in a mess. By the time they are 7, they should be learning their tables. They should know their tables by the time they are about 8.

However, the National Curriculum requirements for knowing multiplication facts are different from Ann's wishes. It is not until Level 4, which is what the average 11-year-old is expected to know, understand and be able to use, that knowledge and use of all tables up to 10x10 will be assessed. 'Parrot-fashion' learning of tables will not develop understanding of the number patterns in multiplication and division. The conversation continued with discussion about the twins' mental skills in calculation.

Ann: They do do some at school. We practice this on the way to school. I don't really know if it's coming from school or what we do at home.

Interviewer: As parents, how much do you feel the school does to help you understand what your children are doing?

Ann: We see the teachers once a term. Staff are more approachable if they know you. Possibly because I helped at the middle school for so long, I can go in and ask questions but the other parents don't feel they can.

Interviewer: If the school ran some parent education evenings would you go?

Paul: We did when we lived in the other county. The school was very approachable.

Interviewer: What do you want to know about your children's mathematics?

Paul: Well, we're not actually aware of the syllabus, of what they're doing throughout the year.

Interviewer: Do you help them at home?

Paul: I've got maths books from O-level up to ONC level. So we've got a few books available. One of our children got in a tizzy over fractions so I sat down with him and explained it to him. Basically, he didn't really understand. Once he got the idea he found it quite easy. It seemed to me that it hadn't really been explained to him, but we don't really know what they're doing, do we? They come with their homework problems but we're not really aware of what they'll be doing next. There's no feedback from the school.

Ann and Paul do not feel able to approach their sons' schools in order to ask for further information about their children's work in mathematics, nor do they have much information about the mathematics curriculum, what children will learn and when. Do other parents have similar feelings about mathematics teaching and, perhaps more importantly, about their children's school? This raises the question of how to ensure that parents receive adequate information about their children's programme of work, of the teaching methods to be employed, and of the content of the National Curriculum. Some excellent suggestions for encouraging parental involvement in mathematics can be found in the Mathematical Association publication 'Sharing Mathematics with Parents' (1987b). Many primary schools have set up parent education evenings so that there are opportunities for parents to try for themselves some of the mathematics which their children experience. Other schools have open days, so that parents can see their children at work.

Teachers in some schools have tried to use the children's interest in their work to foster home-school links. In Chapter 5, Elizabeth Jones, in 'Mathematical Investigations' describes how she developed stronger home-school links through investigations which the children took home to share with their families. The children in her class were very excited about this new approach which involved home as well as schools; some of the children reported that the investigations which they had enjoyed the most were the ones which they had taken home to share with their families.

Many adults regard mathematics as hard, as a subject at which they failed at school. This can be seen in some of the teachers' contributions in this book. The following extract from a conversation with a hospital nurse, who has an 11-year-old daughter, exemplifies many parents' attitudes towards mathematics.

CASE STUDY

Maths is hard. My daughter says it's easy. She's not working very hard at school and is making very slow progress in maths. She's reached Level 3, which is below average for her age. Her teacher says she finds it easy. I don't think she's being challenged. Not if she finds it easy. You have to work really hard in maths, because it progresses and gets harder. If it isn't hard then you're not learning anything.

Yes, mathematics should be challenging. There should be progression. But, for children to become competent mathematicians they do also need to enjoy their work, to enjoy the challenge of an investigation which is 'hard', and to develop personal qualities which ensure that they respond to the challenge. If parents are involved in their children's learning, if parents understand why teachers teach topics differently from how they were taught, then there will be shared understanding of the purpose of the children's learning. There will also be support for the children who will receive similar messages from home and school about their learning.

School governors are consulted about the curriculum. The following is an extract from an interview with someone who has been a school governor for many years and is currently chairperson of one primary school governing body and a governor for another primary school. He was asked for his views about mathematics teaching in primary schools since the introduction of the National Curriculum, but answered in more general terms.

CASE STUDY

Governor: In my role as a governor of a primary school what I know is that the National Curriculum is virtually unmanageable. It is too unwieldy. Too much is being asked of teachers.

Interviewer: Do you believe that you should be able to influence the content of the National Curriculum?

Governor: No. I don't think governors are the appropriate group. But I do think governors represent one of the constituencies which should be consulted, listened to. The governors hear the reality of the situation in schools. Part of the governors' responsibilities is to have an Institutional Development Plan. This reflects our priorities for the next year. We try to see that this deals with resources like textbooks and inservice needs for the staff. We tend to take the advice of the head; if the pressure is on for more history that year then that is our priority too. We, as governors, don't come with curriculum expertise. We do need to see that all areas of the curriculum are being covered. We need to see that there is a policy. Teachers have got it hard enough anyway. If governors started asking questions about the National Curriculum this would just cause more stress. At the end of each year I talk, with the head, with each post-holder. This is to review whether they need governor policies to do with resources.

Development of understanding between teachers and school governors will help teachers to fulfil needs. These can be INSET needs, resources, or the needs to revise and implement the school's policy for mathematics teaching. All of these will need funding in order to assist their effective implementation and evaluation. Encouragement of governors to visit school in order to see children at work can help further governor understanding of how children are taught mathematics, of the benefits of developing the skills associated with problem-solving and enquiry, and of the use of calculators and IT within mathematics teaching and learning.

Teacher confidence in the mathematics curriculum

From contributions in this book has come an impression of teachers who lack confidence in their own ability as mathematicians and who also had poor experiences of mathematics as learners. A group of primary PGCE students were asked to record their experiences of mathematics as learners.

CASE STUDY

Emma: I did what was called 'discovery' maths at school. It involved things like walking around the school with trundle wheels, working out the area of the school, measuring the playground, lots of building shapes and 3D shapes. I can't remember much before I was 8. I remember being taught to tell the time. I can remember thinking, 'That's five minutes! That's how you tell the time. That's what they mean'. I can remember maths at secondary school. I was taught by Dr H... who was really frightening. Maths was in absolute dead silence. Double maths on a Wednesday and sitting there and just being so terrified of giving the wrong answer, of saying anything which would make him annoyed. He was completely unapproachable. Thinking back I was just so frightened of that man. I can remember still being up at 2 o'clock in the morning with my homework and still not understanding it and being too frightened to say. I got O-Level but that was because I learnt how to do it. I could remember the method. I memorized the method.

Helen: At primary school we worked from maths books. I can just remember one page was about measuring with hand spans. I can just remember going around measuring big things like tables. It was good fun. It was a real change to secondary school from primary school. When you get to secondary school you're streamed.

Sarah: At secondary school I enjoyed maths. I didn't find it too difficult. The whole setting was all right so I just went through and did well. But there were people in the same group who didn't enjoy maths.

These students have all achieved at least a GCSE grade 3 or its equivalent in mathematics, in order to become teachers. However, both Emma and Helen lack confidence in their mathematical ability; only Sarah is confident. Past experience of failure in mathematics can have a lasting, detrimental effect upon teachers' self-confidence in mathematics teaching. The fast rate of change since 1989 with the introduction of the National Curriculum may have compounded the sense of inadequacy that many teachers express about mathematics. So much that is new to many schools has been introduced, with new approaches to teaching which involve children in decision-making, in prediction, in long investigations.

Some mathematics content, such as probability, the range of data-handling techniques, the use of calculators and Logo, are also new to many schools.

During conversation with the governor, Ann and Paul's lack of awareness about the mathematics curriculum and their unwillingness to approach their children's schools for more details were discussed.

CASE STUDY

Governor: I've talked to many people about their children's education. What comes over quite strongly is that parents feel they daren't ask their children's teachers anything serious about the curriculum because the teachers seem so frightened and any question is seen as a threat. You just get on better if you don't ask anything. Teachers are scared of being shown up to be wrong.

If this is true, teachers need to be supported in their work, so that it is possible for parents to approach teachers to ask about the curriculum and current methods of teaching mathematics. The over-reliance upon the workbook or workcard approach to teaching mathematics reflects teachers' insecurities with the content. However, the teachers who contributed to this book, using different approaches, also felt insecure. Opportunities for inservice had helped them gain enough confidence to identify aspects of their teaching which they wanted to change and to introduce new approaches within their classroom. Not only were they successful in their own classrooms but there was value added in that they saw opportunities for extending what they had achieved through the interest of other teachers and through the development of school policy.

The role of the mathematics coordinator is of vital importance in the mathematical development of the school. Whereas some of the teachers who produced case studies were coordinators for mathematics, many were not. They had been encouraged to attend an inservice course and then to undertake some classroom research. Winteridge (1989) points to the importance of the coordinator as monitor of the mathematics teaching throughout the school, and supporter of the positive contributions which individual staff can make to school development of mathematics.

Where teachers are confident or have the support of colleagues, then exciting developments are more likely to occur. From teachers' contributions in Chapter 2, it can be seen that for the more confident teacher there are possibilities for involving parents more closely in their children's mathematics through the use of maths trails. The development of cooperative involvement of parents, teachers and children through a local maths trail can enhance understanding by parents of the mathematics curriculum and how it is taught. Where this happens, the comment of the governor about teacher confidence will become redundant as teachers and parents learn to place trust in each other.

A welcoming school environment, with attractive displays which include examples of children's work, can do much to improve teacher and parent relationships. Good display does much to commend the work which children have undertaken; it is also a means for showing teaching methods. Children's own methods of recording, which may involve individual pencil and paper methods for calculation, can be displayed. Parents and other visitors to the school then have the opportunity to see what children have achieved, to follow the processes and skills which children have used. Results displayed from an investigation can help to demonstrate that often in mathematics there is no 'right' answer, but a range of solutions to a problem, some of which may be deemed to be more sophisticated than others.

Ways forward

This section suggests means for improving teacher confidence, which will come through more understanding of the nature and purpose of teaching mathematics and of the means to achieve good quality teaching and learning.

Understanding the curriculum

If teacher confidence in teaching mathematics is to be improved, there has to be clarification of the content of the mathematics curriculum. Teachers of Year 2 children have been involved in agreement trials where samples of children's work are compared in order to agree interpretations of the statements of attainment. This has been done as an attempt to meet the need for standardized assessment procedures across England and Wales.

Two teachers in Chapter 6 discussed the need for agreement about the meaning of statements of attainments across a school and others in the locality. However, this is rather like putting the cart before the horse, as the teaching which could lead to such assessments being made has not been considered. In order to improve teacher confidence it would be helpful to have teacher discussions on the programmes of study. These would consider the implications of the programmes of study, including the range of experiences which are implied in, for example,

learning and using multiplication facts up to 5x5 and all those in the 2, 5 and 10 multiplication tables (PoS from Ma2/3).

Identification of experiences which fit within this programme of study, which contribute towards children learning these tables and being able to use the table facts would be beneficial. Discussion about the use of pegboard arrays, the calculator as an aid in learning and checking table facts, dice games, identification of multiplication patterns from number lines and number squares, and development of quick recall of table facts, will lead to clearer understanding of the range of experiences which will benefit children's learning and of the nature of learning, of how to help children to build their knowledge and understanding, and of possible routes for progression.

Children who are engaged in the experiences listed above will also be involved in aspects of Ma1. For example:

investigating and testing predictions, and general statements
checking results, considering whether they are sensible

(PoS from Ma1/3)

Practical activities which involve generating multiplication patterns will encourage children to predict, to make generalizations, to compare their results with others, and to see if their results fit within their expected pattern. Thus, consideration of any part of the PoS from Ma 2 to 5 needs to involve Ma1 as well. Using and Applying Mathematics permeates the mathematics curriculum, so that children have the opportunity to use what they know in context (applications strand), talk about their work, find appropriate ways of recording what they have done (mathematics communication strand) make and test predictions and form generalizations (reasoning, logic and proof strand).

From understanding of the implications of the programmes of study it is likely that there will follow agreement about the indications for attainment. What constitutes proof of attainment can be developed from discussions about the range of experiences implied within the PoS.

Planning for teaching and learning

Once there is clarification about the PoS and of possible routes for progression and development, then planning for teaching and learning becomes more manageable. The topic versus single subject debate was rehearsed in Chapter 5. From teachers' evidence of the effectiveness of their approaches to teaching, what was seen to be of paramount importance was the clarity of teaching and learning objectives.

The majority of primary schools use a published scheme to support their mathemactics teaching. Recently published schemes have used the National Curriculum mathematics, others take a wider view of mathematics and try to ensure that they have a framework within which the National Curriculum, and its possible revisions, will fit. Most schools also have a bank of materials which supplement their scheme and which also support topics where their chosen scheme is weak. Evidence from the CAN project (Shuard, *et al.*, 1991) shows that as teachers involved in the project became more self-confident in their mathematics teaching they, in general, placed less reliance upon published schemes. However, the project teachers had a high level of support from advisory teachers and through regular meetings between teachers involved in the project. As teacher confidence grows, it is to be hoped that such heavy reliance upon schemes, particularly those which encourage the children to race through their workbooks, will diminish and teachers will become more discerning in the resource materials they choose.

Children need to experience both activities which allow for open outcomes, for example, some investigations where there will be a range of possible solutions, and also those activities where there is a 'right' answer, such as opportunities to practise using a new number skill. Experiencing both types gives children opportunities to acquire knowledge, to practise using newly acquired skills and to develop problem-solving skills and strategies. Activities which have open outcomes can be used for a mixed ability group, whereas the latter are more likely to be suitable for children of similar ability.

There must be concern for those student teachers who report earlier in this chapter on the poor models of teaching which they met in school. This would seem to be linked to teacher confidence in their own mathematical understanding and their ability to identify a suitable learning programme for their pupils. With more time being spent in schools by student teachers, there must be quality of experience for students as learners as well as children as learners.

Teacher assessment and record-keeping

Clarification of the programmes of study leads to understanding of the implications within the statements of attainment. For example:

'Recognise different types of movement' (Ma4/2b)

involves children's understanding of rotation and translation, and of angle. All of this is implied within that one SoA. Collection of evidence of experience and understanding of each individual component implied by this SoA would be far too time-consuming; however, an assessment activity which allows children to show that they can use translation, rotation and knowledge of angle, in order to move themselves, a programmable toy or screen turtle graphics, would enable such an assessment to be made.

Careful assessment enables children's attainments to be monitored and for the next stage of learning to be identified. Clear, unambiguous record-keeping is necessary in order to inform all the partners involved in a child's education, including the child, parents and the receiving teacher or school. In order for such records to be accessible to other teachers, the need for shared understanding about what is involved in assessing a particular SoA is paramount.

Whole-school development

Teachers have described small-scale classroom projects which involved them in developing new aspects of teaching and learning. Within these projects one important aspect has been that of evaluation of the effectiveness of what has been trialled and, where it has been developed further, the monitoring of future progress. In order to improve teacher confidence in mathematics teaching there is a need for much more whole-school development to be undertaken. However, in Chapter 6 one strong message from mathematics coordinators was that mathematics has been developed and now it is the turn of other curriculum areas - a message which conflicts with others from the same coordinators pointing to teachers' lack of confidence in teaching mathematics and the need for continuing support and further training. What this message does suggest is that the pressure for development of the nine subjects of the National Curriculum is immense and that there is not enough time for continuing development in each subject area. The governor commented upon this.

CASE STUDY

In my role as a governor of a primary school what I know is that the National Curriculum is virtually unmanageable. It is too unwieldy. Too much is being asked of teachers.

This comment reflects current thinking from teacher associations and from the NCC which is considering how to make the statutory curriculum more manageable. The size of the National Curriculum makes it unwieldy and very difficult to teach effectively. The discussion that follows takes note of the enormous pressures from all the component subject areas upon primary teachers. However, there is still a need for teachers to improve their confidence in mathematics teaching.

If a staff group identifies small, manageable steps for development, ones in which everyone feels that they can take part, then there is a recipe for success from the start. Such small steps might be the development of a maths trail by the mathematics coordinator, which other teachers then use with their classes, or it could be the development of a project pack for a particular aspect of mathematics teaching, such as probability. All teachers could be encouraged to contribute favourite activities or resources which they have found useful. These small steps will take time, but their outcomes are likely to be successful and thus lead to increased confidence in one aspect of mathematics, at least. From this, larger steps can be taken, which can build on the success already achieved.

Successful small-scale development by one or two teachers can lead to the formulation of whole-school development programmes. For such a programme to be successful, teachers will need to agree common goals and an action plan for achieving those goals. It is not sufficient to agree to implement new materials or to change teaching methods - there need to be training sessions and informal help and support for all teachers.

Support from other schools in the neighbourhood can be useful. Other schools may already have developed particular topics and would be willing to discuss the process that they have undergone, to show the resources which they developed and to discuss the benefits and difficulties which their monitoring has identified. Schools with similar needs could work together, particularly smaller schools, so that experiences and expertise can be shared. The introduction of LMS does not mean that such developments should cease, rather that schools within a community can show the community the benefits of cooperation.

Janet C's experience of cross-pyramid development (Chapter 6) shows that much can be achieved through mutual help from teachers from different age phases working together. Teachers of Key Stage 1 children have so much experience of teacher assessment and SATs administration. High school teachers will be able to offer IT support. Throughout the system it would be possible to set up a loan system for resources, which can be useful for evaluation of the resource before a school commits money to buying its own, or it can be used for resources which are not needed very often, so that schools can share these if appropriate. Within the pyramid structure lies the opportunity to develop understanding of programmes of study, of statements of attainment, and to share successful teaching strategies.

The NCET (1991) project identifies the importance of shared objectives and of clear channels for communication between all of those involved. This is important whether it is whole-school development or the involvement of a number of schools.

From the evidence collected from teachers, a strong case can be made for inservice courses for mathematical development. There are two forms of inservice: one is for all teachers within a school, which can be led by the school's mathematics coordinator, and will either address a particular need which teachers have identified, or will be to begin the process of identifying avenues of development; the other form of inservice is offered by LEAs or higher education institutions. These courses are for individual teachers as part of their professional development programme. The small amount of school budgets available for funding teachers on courses means that few teachers are able to take advantage of this form of professional development. However, meeting other, like-minded teachers, away from the school environment, who will most probably share anxieties about their competence in teaching of mathematics, can offer support. The opportunity to discuss the teaching situation, in confidence, allows teachers to hear of others' experiences, and to learn about innovative teaching methods, content and new resources. Teachers can try out new materials, develop their practice and evaluate their achievements.

The second form of inservice, which allows teachers to stand back from their school situation and to reflect upon their practice, needs to be seen as part of a whole-school development programme. Time must be available within the school's development programme for dissemination of new ideas gained from sources external to the school, so that the feasibility of introducing new developments can be considered.

Conclusion

This chapter has considered the achievements in primary mathematics teaching and learning since the introduction of the National Curriculum. In some schools there have been major changes in teaching methods and in the content of the curriculum. The main recommendations for future developments are:

- shared understanding of the implications of the programmes of study;
- shared understanding of the meanings of the statements of attainment;
- identification of teaching objectives, careful planning, assessment and record-keeping;
- the need for further development of the curriculum through whole-school and pyramid support;
- individual professional development programmes, away from the school environment.

The following quotation from the final report of the National Curriculum Working Group: Mathematics (DES, 1988a) offers hope for future achievement in mathematics by all children:

Mathematics is not only taught because it is useful. It should be a source of delight and wonder, offering pupils intellectual excitement, for example, in the discovery of relationships, the pursuit of rigour and the achievement of elegant solutions. Pupils should also appreciate the essential creativity of mathematics: it is a live subject which is continuously evolving as technology and the needs of society evolve.

Bibliography

Alexander, R., Rose, J. and Woodhead, C. (1992) *Curriculum Organisation and Classroom Practice in Primary Schools. A discussion paper*, London: Department of Education and Science.

Ahston P. *et al.* (1975) *Aims into Practice in the Primary School*, London: Hodder and Stoughton.

Association for Science Education, Association of Teachers of Mathematics, Mathematical Association, National Association of Teachers of English (1989) *The National Curriculum: Making it work in the primary school*, Hatfield: ASE.

Bell, L. and Day C. (1991) *Managing the Professional Development of Teachers*, Buckingham: Open University

Booth, W., Briten, P. and Scott, F. (1987) *Themes Familiar. Research and display in the primary school using everyday objects*, Twickenham: Belair Publications.

Brissenden, T. (1988) *Talking about Mathematics. Mathematical Discussion in Primary Classrooms*, Oxford: Basic Blackwell.

Bruce, T. (1987) *Early Childhool Education*, London: Hodder and Stoughton.

Burton, L. (1984) *Thinking Things Through*, Oxford: Basil Blackwell.

Cambridge Mathematics (1991) *Module 5. Set 2 Extension Activities*, Cambridge: Cambridge University Press.

Cockcroft, W. (1982) *Mathematics Counts*, Report of the Committee of Inquiry into the Teaching of Mathematics in Schools under the Chairmanship of Dr W.H. Cockcroft, London: HMSO.

Connor, C. (1991) *Assessment and Testing in the Primary School*, London: Falmer Press.

Day, C., Johnston, D. and Whitaker, P. (1985) *Managing Primary Schools. A professional development approach*, London: Harper and Row.

Department of Education and Science (1978) *Primary Education in England*, London: HMSO.

Department of Education and Science (1985a) *The Curriculum from 5–16, Curriculum Matters 2*, London: HMSO.

Department of Education and Science (1985b) *Mathematics from 5 to 16, Curriculum Matters 3*, London: HMSO.

Department of Education and Science (1987a) *National Curriculum Mathematics Working Group, Interim Report*, London: DES.

Department of Education and Science (1987b) *The National Curriculum 5 to 16. A consultation document*, London: DES.

Department of Education and Science (1988a) *Mathematics for ages 5 to 16*, proposals of the Secretary of State for Education and Science and the Secretary of State for Wales, London: Central Office of Information.

Department of Education and Science (1988b) *National Curriculum Task Group on Assessment and Testing: a report*, London: DES.

208

Department of Education and Science (1989a) *Mathematics in the National Curriculum*, London: HMSO.

Department of Education and Science (1989b) *National Curriculum. From policy to practice*, London: HMSO.

Department of Education and Science (1990) *Technology in the National Curriculum*, London: HMSO.

Department of Education and Science (1991a) *Mathematics for ages 5 to 16*, proposals of the Secretary of State for Education and Science and the Secretary of State for Wales, London: Central Office of Information.

Department of Education and Science (1991b) *Mathematics in the National Curriculum*, London: HMSO.

Desforges, C. and Cockburn, A. (1987) *Understanding the Mathematics Teacher. A study of practice in first schools*, London: Falmer Press.

Domoney, B., Gash, P., Harrison, P., James, L., Sawyer, A. and Wright, D. (1991). *Nelson Mathematics*, Walton-on-Thames: Thomas Nelson.

Gipps, C. (1990) *Assessment. A teacher's guide to the issues*, London: Hodder and Stoughton.

Graham, A. (1991) 'Where is the 'P' in statistics?', in Pimm, D. and Love, E. (eds) *Teaching and Learning School Mathematics*, Sevenoaks: Hodder and Stoughton for The Open University.

Hatch, G. (1984) *Bounce to it*, Manchester: Manchester Polytechnic.

Haylock, D. and Cockburn, A. (1989) *Understanding Early Years Mathematics*, London: Paul Chapman Publishing.

Her Majesty's Inspectors (1989) *Aspects of Primary Education. The teaching and learning of mathematics*, London: HMSO.

Her Majesty's Inspectors (1991) *The Implementation of the Curricular Requirements of the Education Reform Act. Assessment, recording and reporting, a report by HMI Inspectorate on the first year, 1989-90*, London: HMSO.

Her Majesty's Inspectors (1992) *The Implementation of the Curricular Requirements of the Education Reform Act. Assessment, recording and reporting. A report by HMI Inspectorate on the Second Year, 1990-1991*. London: HMSO.

Hohmann, M., Banet, B. and Weikhart, D. (1979) *Young Children in Action. A manual for preschool educators*, Ypsilanti: High/Scope Press.

Hughes, M. (1986) *Children and Number Difficulties in Learning Mathematics*, Oxford: Blackwell.

Kelly, A.V. (ed.) (1984) *Microcomputers and the Curriculum*, London: Harper and Row.

Lloyd-Jones, A. (1992) 'Clent Maths Day', *Mathematics Round the Country*, 36, Spring Term, pp. 6-7.

Lloyd-Jones, R. and Bray, E. (1986) *Assessment from Principles to Action* Basingstoke: Macmillan.

Love, E. and Tahta, D. (1991) 'Reflections on some words used in mathematics education', in Pimm, D. and Love, E. (eds) *Teaching and Learning School Mathematics*, Sevenoaks: Hodder and Stoughton for The Open University.

The Mathematical Association (1987a) *Maths Talk*, Cheltenham: Stanley Thornes.

The Mathematical Association (1987b) *Sharing Mathematics with parents, Planning school-based events*, Cheltenham: Stanley Thornes.

The Mathematical Association (1988) *Managing Mathematics. A handbook for the Head of Department*, Cheltenham: Stanley Thornes.

Maths Development Team (1988) *Developing Mathematics in Your Classroom*, Worcester: Hereford and Worcester Education Department.

Maths Development Team (1990) *Mathematics in Action*, Worcester: Hereford and Worcester Education Department.

Matthews, G. and Matthews, J. (project directors) (1990) *Early Mathematical Experiences*, 3rd edn. A Schools Curriculum Council Project, Harlow: Longman for SCDC Publications.

National Council for Educational Technology (1991) *Promoting Curriculum Continuity between Primary and Secondary Schools*, Warwick: NCET.

National Curriculum Council (1988) *Mathematics in the National Curriculum*, A report to the Secretary of State for Education on the statutory consultation for attainment targets and programmes of study in mathematics, York: NCC.

National Curriculum Council (1989) *Mathematics Non-Statutory Guidance*, York: NCC.

National Curriculum Council (1991) *Mathematics Non-Statutory Guidance*, York: NCC.

National Curriculum Council (1992) *Using and Applying Mathematics. Books A and B*, York: NCC.

Papert, S. (1981) *Mindstorms: Children, computers and powerful ideas*, Brighton: Harvester Press.

Reid, I. and Rushton, J. (eds.) (1985) *Teachers, Computers and Classrooms*, Manchester: Manchester University Press.

Richards, C. (1985) 'The primary curriculum: perennial questions and general issues', in Richards, C. (ed.) *The Study of Primary Education: A Source Book Volume 2*, London: Falmer Press.

Salinger, M. and Baker, L. (1991) *The What, Why, How and When of Mathematics Trails*, Derby: Association of Teachers of Mathematics.

Scholastic (1989) *Brainwaves*, Leamington Spa: Scholastic.

Schools Council (1983) *Primary Practice - Schools Council Working Paper 75*, London: Methuen Educational.

Schools Examination and Assessment Council (1990) *Assessment Matters: No 3. APU Mathematics Monitoring 1984-1988 (Phase 2). A summary of findings, conclusions and implications*, based on work by the Assessment of Performance Unit, London: HMSO.

Schools Examination and Assessment Council (1992) *The Evaluation of National Curriculum Assessment at Key Stage 1* (ENCA 1 Project), London: Central Office of Information.

Scottish Office Education Department (SOED) (1991) *Curriculum and Assessment in Scotland, National Guidelines, Mathematics 5-14*, Edinburgh: HMSO.

210

Senior, S. (1989) *Using IT across the National Curriculum*, Sittingbourne: Owlet Books.

Shuard, H. (1986) *Primary Mathematics Today and Tomorrow*, Harlow: Longman.

Shuard, D., Walsh, A., Goodwin, J. and Worcester, V. (1991) *Calculators, Children and Mathematics*, The PrIME Project, Hemel Hempstead: Simon and Schuster.

Skemp, R. (1989) *Mathematics in the Primary School*, London: Routledge.

Stocker, J. (1990) *Assessing and Recording Achievement: Some examples from primary schools*, Leicester: Leicestershire Education Authority.

Straker, A. (1989) *Children Using Computers*, Oxford: Blackwell.

Underwood, J.D.M. and Underwood, G. (1990) *Computers and Learning. Helping children acquire thinking skills*, Oxford: Blackwell.

Walsh, A. (1991) 'The calculator as a tool for learning', in Pimm, D. and Love, E. (eds) *Teaching and Learning School Mathematics*, Sevenoaks: Hodder and Stoughton for The Open University.

Whitaker, P. (1984) *The Process of Change*, Leicester: Personal Learning Associates.

Williams, E. and Shuard, H. (1987) *Primary Mathematics Today*, Harlow: Longman.

Winteridge, D.J. (ed.) *A Handbook for Primary Mathematics Coordinators*, London: Paul Chapman Publishing.

Resources

Cambridge Mathematics (1991) *Module 5. Set 2 Extension Activities*, Cambridge: Cambridge University Press.

Centre for Language in Primary Education (1990) *Mathematics Record. Draft*, Southwark: CLPE.

Domoney, B., Gash, P., Harrison, P., James, L., Sawyer, A. and Wright, D. (1991). *Nelson Mathematics*, Walton-on-Thames: Thomas Nelson.

Lift Off with Numbers, available from ESM, Abbeygate House, East Road, Cambridge, CB1 1DB.

Logotron Logo, available from Logotron Ltd. Dales Brewery, Gwydir Street, Cambridge CB1 2LJ.

PIP, available from Swallow Systems, 32 High Street, High Wycombe, Bucks HP11 2AQ.

PODD, available from ESM, Abbeygate House, East Road, Cambridge CB1 1DB.

Stylus, available from Prime Resources, 6 Sunbury Avenue, Newcastle upon Tyne NE2 3HE.

Valiant Roamer, available from Valiant Technology Ltd, Gulf House, 370 Old York Road, Wandsworth, London SW18 15P.

Index

214